TRUE TALES OF GHOSTS & GALES

Mysterious Great Lakes Shipwrecks

by Wes Oleszewski

Avery Color Studios, Inc.
Gwinn, Michigan

ISBN 1-892384-21-3

Library of Congress Control Number: 2002117857

First Edition 2003

Published by
Avery Color Studios, Inc.
Gwinn, Michigan 49841

Cover artwork by:
Ship painting by Captain C. (Bud) Robinson,
Ships On Canvas
Photo by Eric Treece

To Bobby McGarrity,

"My cousin Bobby", an all around good guy who really deserves to have a book dedicated to him.

Table of Contents

Foreword

When the wind blows and the lakes churn, the waves that are created come marching ashore and explode upon the land. In a rhythm of thunder they announce that another storm has come to the lakes. Standing on the shore and feeling the wind clawing at your face while having your thoughts nearly drowned out by the roar of the waves, it is easy to imagine the countless other times that such storms have come calling. Indeed when you do that, make sure that you stretch your imagination as far as it will go, because there have been thousands of gales on the Great Lakes and from them have come tens of thousands of true tales. From these true tales occasionally there comes the story of a ghost or two. These things seem to go together like the wind causing the waves.

There are in fact, so many tales that no one can research and tell them all. In this book we will try to look closely at an assortment of those events. We will examine in great detail the very obscure true tales and along the way we will experience some ghosts and gales.

As in all of my other books, everything that you read within this text is true. If I could not find proof of an event recorded in writing, then I will tell you that no record exists. Whenever possible I have tried to cross-check the statements made concerning each event by using at least two independent sources. Thus when you read of a ghostly appearance or of a ghastly shipwreck you will know, without doubt, that the story is factual. For example, in one case a little girl who was originally described in the records simply as "The captain's little granddaughter" had a sighting that I needed to document. Still, I could not begin to tell her story until I learned her name. Perhaps this seems like a small detail, but details are what I do best. The problem was, how do you track down a three year old girl who lived in Ogdensburg, New York in 1869? With a bit of census sifting and some detective know how I discovered Jennie B. Houghton and thus could then tell her story. I had the same problem with a little boy in Milwaukee from the year 1873. In that case, I engaged the assistance of Suzette Lopez of the Milwaukee Public Library as well as visiting that facility myself, and still we were unable to locate his name. So, you will find him here listed simply as "Henry Valentine's little boy." I could have made up a name, as some other authors would do, but that would be a disservice to his memory.

The only occasion when I deviated from the rule of written proof is when occasional dialogue was synthesized in order to better tell the tale. Not all dialogue in this book has been synthesized, however. Whenever I found quoted verbiage in publication I have tried to use it. The exception to that rule being that whenever the quoted statement appears to have obviously been concocted by the publication that printed it, the quote was dismissed.

Not all of the tales contained within this book involve ghost stories. Many involve shipwrecks and adventures on the lakes. It is this mixture of ghosts and gales that makes the reading of each chapter fun. Of course you, the reader, have the least fun of our two jobs. My job, as the author, involves the discovery of the "whole" story and finding of the lost facts and that is more fun. Then I get to write it all down and share it with you and that is the most fun of all.

On the darker side, it is important to keep in mind that all of the people that we will learn about in this book were real. They were actual living, breathing folks who had hopes and dreams just as you and I have. They had friends who knew them and kin who loved them. Some were historic figures of their era who have long since been forgotten while others were just regular people who happened to make their living sailing the Great Lakes.

Lastly, in the research and documentation of history, we sometimes find that what is thought to be written fact today, can change tomorrow. History is as changeable as the people who lived it and what the documents say today can be later disproved by a discovery of additional events. We must always be willing to look at an event and say that we thought we had it right, but we were mistaken, and then we have to be able to correct ourselves. Overall, I can say that if I have made a mistake, I will correct it and if a story needs to be rewritten I will do that too. What is important is that I have taken these forgotten people and shipwrecks and brought them to your attention, and that you had fun reading these true tales of ghosts and gales.

A Voice In The Fog

By the afternoon of Sunday, August 6, 2000 the fog that had set in at Grand Haven, Michigan was showing no signs of lifting. Out on Lake Michigan the conditions were just as thick with the visibility ranging from one quarter of a mile to one half mile. Overall it was a murky end to a fairly festive week in the harbor. The previous six days had been used to celebrate the annual Coast Guard Festival in that port city and the entire week had been dedicated to the keepers of valor–the United States Coast Guard. In attendance at the festival was the 180 foot buoy tender *Acacia*, the 140 foot ice-breaking tugs *Neah Bay* and *Mobile Bay* and most prominently, the flagship of the Great Lakes Coast Guard, the mighty 290 foot ice breaker *Mackinaw*. During daylight hours, the Coast Guard fleet was open to tours as proud crew members stood by. Of course all good times must come to an end, and so it was with the annual Coast Guard Festival. Now the vessels and crews who had attended the event would return to their normal work. On that foggy Sunday the *Mackinaw* cast off her lines and headed out to attend to her duties.

Moving into the cotton fog the *Mackinaw* had her radar scanning the distance and extra crew were stationed on her deck to keep a sharp lookout. In fact every crewman on duty was keeping a weather eye toward the lake. It would really look bad if while departing the Coast Guard festival, the pride of the lakes Coast Guard, were to accidentally run down some unsuspecting pleasure craft in the fog. With that in mind, the pilothouse crew inched the big ice breaker silently across the glassy surface of Lake Michigan using all of the caution of a jeweler working on a fine watch. Well out onto Lake Michigan the big steel hull of the *Mackinaw* slid along the surface making little more than a ripple as her commander directed her to be steered to the northwest. Like every other member of the crew onboard the *Mackinaw* at that moment, the pilothouse watch had no idea that resting just over 100 feet beneath them were the bones of a long forgotten wooden lakeboat. Also resting beneath them were the memories and the spirits of a tragic morning long ago when a scene of disaster was played out upon these same waters. It was a memory that would soon reach out and touch all of those aboard the *Mackinaw* in a haunting manner.

Just eight and one half miles northwest of Grand Haven, a crewman standing lookout heard a sudden cry coming from the lake. For a moment he thought he was mistaken, but then the voice cried out again. It was the voice of a child, the voice of a little boy out there in the distant fog, crying for help. Instantly the crew of the *Mackinaw* were called to alert and all off-duty personnel were mustered on deck. Now the voice was heard again and it was certainly that of a little boy calling for help.

As with their predecessors in the United States Life-Saving Service, it is the sworn duty of every member of the Coast Guard to place their own lives in peril to save the lives of others and now their call to duty had come again. The *Mackinaw* began a standard search pattern as her crew strained their eyes and ears against the fog. Lake Michigan, however, frustrated their efforts and nothing was found. Now Coast Guard station Grand Haven was notified by radio. Once again, like their lifesaving service forerunners, the station's crew manned their boat and charged to the rescue knowing only that somewhere out there a little boy was in the water calling for help. It is important to note that this was the era

Coast Guard ice breaker Mackinaw. *D.J. Story photo.*

before the September 11, 2001 attacks on America and the annual assets budgeted to the Coast Guard were so thin that they were nearly invisible. Deploying a rescue boat meant spending some of those thin assets and this was not an action done on a lark or on a hunch. The Coast Guard was convinced that there was a life in danger. So it was that the swift rescue boat was deployed and it joined the *Mackinaw* in the search. As the second boat arrived on the scene, the little boy's voice was clearly heard again, in the foggy distance calling for help. Now both Coast Guard vessels began to search. Approximately 1,000 yards from the center of the search area, a pleasure craft was found. The occupants of the pleasure boat had no children aboard and had heard nothing of the voice calling for help. Likewise, every other pleasure craft in the vicinity had heard nothing.

In the days that followed, no one reported anyone missing. There were no overdue pleasure craft anywhere on Lake

Michigan and a check of local law enforcement showed no one reporting any loss of a child. All of the Coast Guard vessels returned to their stations and their crews resumed their duties having never found the source of the voice. Officially, the Coast Guard simply states that "The case remains open." Officially, the Coast Guard can offer no explanation for the events off of Grand Haven on August 6, 2000. That is because they were actually searching in the right place, but in the wrong time. Their deployment of assets was too late …126 years too late.

Along the Milwaukee waterfront the smell of horse manure hung heavy as Harry Lee's boots seemed to avoid the piles of droppings that were common on every street. It was a warm Saturday evening in the late summer of 1873 and Harry was on his way to a favored tavern after a hard day's toil at the Wolf and Davidson shipyard. With a swagger that was befitting his position as a foreman at the shipyard, Harry entered the darkened tavern and bellied up to the bar. Some of the boys on his crew were already there and were also a few sips ahead of their foreman. Flowing faster than the drinks was the grumbling that the shipyard workers were spewing. As Harry's calloused hand gripped his glass he listened intently to the men while they vented. Theirs was a situation that most shipyards would not force upon their workers and could actually be considered a sin. Both Harry Lee and his crew were being forced to, once again, work on Sunday and it was again being caused by one boat, the steamer *Ironsides*.

"I'm getting' mighty tired of workin' Sundays on that rotten *Ironsides*." Harry spouted aloud to a chorus of agreeing groans from his crew. "In the blasted dry dock, replacin' one plank at a time, when her whole stern is rotten."

Harry sneered as he took a long drink and then wiped the excess from his whiskers. His crew grew silent as they waited for their foreman to continue to reflect their disdain.

Around the bar the talk soon resumed with most grumbling being about William H. Wolf and Thomas Davidson themselves. It was their fault for being so greedy as to keep taking the *Ironsides* in for these patch-up jobs. After all, the yard was well on its way toward its best year ever with the building of a tug, a steamer and six schooners, the bosses still insisted on taking these patch-up jobs. Everyone involved would lose their Sundays just so Wolf and Davidson could get that $1,000 for use of the dry dock. Foreman Lee, however, had other thoughts as he gazed toward the bottom of his glass. He knew that the real blame should be focused on Engelmann Transportation and the penny-pinching Engelmanns.

"I'll tell ya' somethin' else." Harry blurted out, again silencing his crew's grumbling "She'll go down soon because of those leaks in her stern." The crew growled in their agreement–"Then old Engelmann will get his due and the yard will be rid of both the *Ironsides* and her Sunday repair jobs."

Such scorn had not always been associated with the *Ironsides*. In fact prior to her employ in the hands of the Engelmann Transportation Company, the vessel was considered as being one of the finest on the lakes and that was a reputation that she still carried with the those who were not involved in her maintenance. When the boat entered service in 1864 she was one of the "Palace Steamers" whose job it was to carry immigrants west at minimal expense, yet carry the wealthy across the same waters in the greatest of luxury. Constructed at the Quayle and Martin yard in Cleveland, she measured 231 feet in length, 38 feet in beam and 14 feet in depth of hold. All of that girth gave her a registered tonnage listed as 937. Erected upon her deck at each of her beam ends were two huge arches, each reinforced with heavy iron plates and bolts. Between the arches, cross-beams extended to fastened the hogging structure as a single unit. Her first class cabins were designed to put any four star hotel to shame. Splendid furniture with velvet covered cushions stocked every room, the floors of which were covered in plush Brussels carpeting. A total of 44 staterooms graced her lines and a large number of those rooms could be turned into family rooms. In the extreme forward end of the boat was located a series of community washrooms. These were all graced with marble fixtures plus a feature, that for this era simply sang out with elegance–hot and cold running water. Another opulent feature was a room for taking baths. It too was equipped with hot and cold running water. On her deck, was located her main cabin with its grand hall saloon that ran nearly the length of the vessel. This room was an open hall that was used for both dining and socializing. At the aft end of the grand hall was a huge painting of the frigate *Ironsides* rendering aid to burning British vessel. At the forward end of the grand hall was another huge painting. That second painting was of the Sault Rapids and the surrounding landscape. This image was in tribute to her designed route of service which would be from the lower lakes through the Saint Marys River and Soo locks into Lake Superior. She would pass the Sault Rapids each time that she passed through the locks.

Propulsion equipment of the *Ironsides* was supplied power from two huge boilers, each of which measured 21 feet long and 10 feet in diameter with 378 water return tubes. She was driven through the water by twin propellers each being nine feet in diameter. All of this appeared to be directed toward the task of moving passengers from the lower lakes to the wilderness ports of the upper lakes with ease and comfort. There was, however a secondary nature to the *Ironsides* at the time of her launching. She was also designed to be an oreboat. Into her sides, companionways had been constructed to allow the rolling on and off of barreled cargoes of iron ore. In 1864 the shipping of iron ore from the upper lakes was still somewhat of a novelty and the quantities that were needed were measured in little more than a few barrels at a time. Still, between ore and the goods that were needed to build the settlements of Lake Superior, freight was as important a cargo to the *Ironsides* as were her passengers. Of course, the boat's crew would do all that they could to insure that the passengers felt that they were aboard a luxury steamer rather than a freighter. From the porters and cooks to the ship's musicians, everyone went out of their way to please the passengers who came aboard the new *Ironsides*.

Indeed the *Ironsides* was a floating palace of the freshwater seas when she was launched. By the time that the boat got into the charge of Engelmann Transportation, however, much of the plushness of her accommodations were becoming worn. Still, her cabins were roomy and she wore her age well as far as the paying public could see.

When the *Ironsides* was constructed, the question of safety was addressed by her initial owners. They had required some state of the art safety features to be added into her design. From hoses for fire fighting to additional lifeboats, she seemed ready to handle any emergency. The vessel's hull was divided into three sections by two "water-tight" bulkheads. Such multiple bulkheads were a rather unusual feature for her day and in 1864 no type of bulkhead was actually "water tight."

Stanton Drawing of the Ironsides. *Author's Collection.*

In less than a decade after her maiden voyage, the *Ironsides* found herself fallen into hard times. Between 1864 and 1873 there were great changes in the Great Lakes maritime industry. In the first years of the 1870s an economic recession had taken place that was bad enough to send some immigrants packing back to the old country. The flood of "pioneers" booking passage to the wilderness of Lake Superior had dwindled to the point where the *Ironsides* was no longer competitive in that trade. She changed hands several times and finally came into the service of the Engelmann Transportation line of Milwaukee. The Engelmann brothers were in an upstart position against the Goodrich Transportation line. For several years they had been in the business of operating a small lumber fleet. Then they acquired a few well worn passenger vessels and transformed themselves into a passenger and freight line. Both the Engelmann Transportation line and the Goodrich Transportation line ran vessels out of Milwaukee to destinations on southern and eastern Lake Michigan. It was short-haul service that carried both passengers and cargo and the competition was cut-throat. Goodrich had the advantage in cash and docks, but Engelmann was determined to beat that edge by using less expensive vessels and saturation schedules. By 1873 the two companies were crisscrossing Lake Michigan, each going to different cities, but each competing for every warm body and cold piece of cargo that could be found around the lake. Along the docks there were those who called Engelmann a skinflint with leaky boats who refused to invest a dime in his fleet. Of course there were those who would say the same about Goodrich. The fact is that this was the era of the robber-barons and it was also the era when there was very little regulation of vessels. Being cast in the role of the "skinflint" could also be the difference between a successful business man and a failure. Using old boats and not investing your profits back into the fleet could spell disaster but could also easily be considered as shrewd. When disaster did strike, there was essentially no government agency to step in and investigate. Although the inspector of steamboats was supposed to do the job, that department was under staffed and under motivated and the Coast Guard would not be established for another four decades. So, normally, a blue ribbon panel would sit down and look into the matter. The members of such panels were usually robber-barons in the same circles as the vessel owner that they were supposed to be investigating. Of course this meant that the game was rigged and the results of the investigation would likely point the finger of blame toward a drown captain rather than his robber-baron boss. Such were the times that found the *Ironsides* coming into Milwaukee harbor on Saturday, September 13, 1873.

Captain Harry Sweetman was nearly beside himself as the vessels hovered up to the dock at Milwaukee's West Water Street. Purser Sam Watkins had orders to see to it that the passengers disembarked only through the forward gangway and not one stick of cargo was to be unloaded until the dock was cleared of passengers. He was also under orders that no stragglers were to be tolerated and every passenger was to be disembarked as swiftly as possible. Captain Sweetman's concern was justified. The *Ironsides* had wet her cargo, again, and he wanted to make sure that the word of this did not get out. News that the boat was in a leaking condition could spread like poison around the port cities of Lake Michigan and could easily cause passengers to avoid her as well as the rest of the Engelmann boats. The fact, however, was that the leaking was so bad that it had gotten ahead of the pumps this time. Now the water in the aft cargo hold was nearly knee deep. By unloading the passengers through the forward gangway, they would not see the flooded compartment or the crew that was working feverishly to pump out the water. By not unloading the damaged cargo, there would be no way for the public to witness that mess either. It was a routine that the crew of the *Ironsides* had been through before.

A phantom leak that no one could seem to find had plagued the *Ironsides* all season. The boat would leak severely when she was under way, but as soon as she was placed into the dry dock, there would be no obvious area found that could cause such an intrusion of water. A few suspected areas would be caulked and a timber or two replaced, but as soon as she was back under power on the open lake, she would begin to take water once again. Although her owners would not face it and her crew did not want to think about it, the fact was that this leak was not in one spot, but along her entire bottom. It is likely that her timbers were springing in almost every butt along her bottom and thus providing for millions of tiny inlets for water. Once the boat was under way, the normal stresses and torques from that activity would have opened up these tiny spots even more and caused a cumulative effect that bordered on her being a sinking vessel. In the dry dock, there would be no apparent sign of a gap that was big enough to cause a major leak. So the best that the repair foremen could do was to patch a suspected location and again tell the company that the boat's entire bottom needed to be repaired. The Engelmann's were simply not willing to invest the down time of the vessel, or the money required to have her entire bottom redone during the busy shipping season. They seemed content to ignore the problem and let the boat keep running.

On the leg prior to the trip that the boat had just completed, she had leaked so badly that her cargo of wheat was damaged. Normally a device known as "Dart's legs" which is a long boom that extends from the elevator into the hold of a vessel is used to unload grain. These legs have a continuous loop belt that has a series of buckets attached and literally chews at the cargo. The grain fills the buckets and is thereby hoisted up into the storage elevator. It works amazingly well on dry grain, but not on wet grain. The damage to the cargo of the *Ironsides* was to the point where the wheat could not be removed from the boat by use of the elevator's Dart legs. Instead the wheat had to be shoveled out by hand and left on the wharf in Grand Haven to dry. Now on her return trip to Milwaukee the package freight had been damaged by the flooding. After the paying passengers had left the dock. The crew set to the task of removing the soaked cargo and placing it on the dock where it would hopefully dry out.

Beyond Captain Sweetman's headaches with the leaking condition of the *Ironsides*, were Chief Engineer Robert McGlue's woes. The leaking was always aft and had a tendency to work its way amidships into his engine room. McGlue and his crew were often working in knee-deep water and having a rough time keeping the boat's fires lit. Still, one who complained too often and too intensely to the front office would likely find himself without a job. In this era of unregulated robber-barons and robber-baron wannabes, such as the Engelmanns, a chief that had been dismissed for such complaints could find himself labeled as "troublesome" and thus unable to find another job on another boat. So, the good chief simply had to be content to grumble to himself in his cabin and tell his crew to just "pump her out" again. Using a combination of her steam pumps and some hand pumps, the crew worked well into Sunday afternoon to get the water out of the *Ironsides*. Then, in the eyes of the Engelmanns, she was ready for more paying passengers, more cargo and another trip across Lake Michigan.

At their small but comfortable home located at 310 Jackson Street, the family of Henry Valentine were just returning from church as the *Ironsides* was preparing to sail again. Henry kept close supervision as his wife changed the clothes of their five year old son from his Sunday best to a cute little blue sailor suit. The garb was indeed proper considering that the little boy and his mother were about to go sailing across Lake Michigan on the *Ironsides*. There would be plenty of time for dinner and then to pack some last minute items before heading out to the Engelmann dock. From their house it was a three block walk to Huron Street and then another three blocks up to the drawbridge and across it to the dock where they would meet the *Ironsides*. For several days the trip on the boat had been the subject of excited conversation between the five year old and his parents and as they left home for the boat, he led the way well ahead in his excitement. As the Valentine family came to the bridge they could see the *Ironsides* docked on the other side of the river.

"There she is," Henry pointed as he half encouraged his son toward the river and half held him safely back. "There's the *Ironsides*, she's the sturdiest boat on the lakes." That is what Henry Valentine wanted to believe. He had worked as a clerk for the Engelmann Transportation line since 1869 and although he had heard the rumors about the leaks he was firmly on the side of the company and knew that the Engelmanns were simply doing what was needed to remain competitive in the market. What he did not know, however, was the extent of the boat's leaking. Henry was also not a marine man by any stretch of the imagination. Having come from a job as a baggage master at the D&M Railroad, his job involved pointy pencils and well maintained ledgers rather than the sea

Stanton Drawing of the Ironsides.
Author's Collection.

worthiness of vessels. To him as well as his five year old son, the *Ironsides* was simply the queen of the fleet.

The five year old gasped in amazement at the *Ironsides* and the riverfront as a whole. It was a nest of activity as vessels of every sort seemed to move in an organized confusion of white steam and black smoke. Tugs pulled schooners and the shores of the river seemed to be a forest of masts. To the left was the Engelmann wharf and to the right of the bridge was the Goodrich dock and it was enough to fill the eyes of a little boy for quite a while. In the middle of it all squatted the *Ironsides* with her gleaming white paint scheme. Excitedly, the Valentine family headed for the dock and the Engelmann Transportation Company's terminal. There was plenty of time as the boat was not scheduled to sail until nine o'clock that night. Still, Henry wanted to get his family securely aboard. He was not going to be making the trip across because his job required that he be at the Engelmann office on Monday morning. So he would send off his family assured in the belief that the *Ironsides* was one of the staunchest boats on the lakes. That was also the perception of the public at large. It was a hard image to argue with as the Valentine family approached the gangway to board the *Ironsides*. Her hefty wooden timbers seemed as strong as the blockhouse of a frontier fort as she sat tightly moored to the wharf. The water between her hull and the wharf was brown and filled with assorted flotsam and a bit of water spouted from a small drain in her side while white steam hissed from unseen locations. Along her boat deck were a series of four lifeboats on each side, a sight that provided assurance that in case of emergency there would be more than enough boats for her passengers and crew. She appeared to be a powerful white sea monster and indeed as staunch as Henry Valentine believed.

At the home of Tim Foley, the perception of the *Ironsides* was quite different that Sunday. Tim was a young, fearless wheelsman employed aboard the *Ironsides*. He had gotten his fill of the leaky boat and had a mind to quit and stay ashore for the remainder of the season because of the boat's rude tendency. When he told First Mate Crosson that he was thinking of going up the street, the mate told him not to be hasty. The company may make it worth his while to stay aboard for the rest of the season. Amazingly, the Engelmanns came across with a raise in pay for Tim if he would agree to remain aboard the *Ironsides*. Considered in the context of the era, this action alone says much about the condition of the vessel. It is almost unheard of for vessel managers in this era to offer increased wages simply to keep a wheelsman. Yet it would indeed be far cheaper to offer crew members another few cents a day to stay on the boat than it would be to lay the boat up and replace her bottom. In context this indicates that the word was out around the waterfront that the *Ironsides* was "tender" and experienced mariners would have nothing to do with her. At his new rate of pay, Tim felt that he could not afford to walk the waterfront looking for another job that would pay the same. This was probably true of other members of the crew who would rather take a raise in pay and also take their chances on the *Ironsides* than go looking for another job. At home Tim expressed his opinion that the boat would not last longer than another "trip or two." His mother implored him to decline the money and stay off of the *Ironsides*, but Tim was sure that he was young enough, savvy enough and strong enough to escape and defy the lake if the vessel went down. Besides, he had just taken his boost in pay and bought a new pair of seven dollar boots, so he had to go back aboard.

Many of the boat's crew saw the regular flooding of the steamer as more of a workplace bother than a danger. One of those crewmen was Second Engineer George Cowen. To him the boat's flooding tendency and the need to constantly pump out the water was simply a disagreeable part of his job. It was all very simple, when the water gets too high in the boat you pump it out. If you get it all, then you get it all, if you don't, then you don't. It was all easier than having to go out and find another job.

It was nearly ten o'clock Sunday evening by the time that the *Ironsides* cast off her lines and departed the dock. Down on the wharf, Henry Valentine waved goodbye as his wife and son waved back. On the walk home he thought of that little sailor suited boy and he wished he could be there with him to share the adventure. Standing at rail of the drawbridge he watched the amber lights of the boat swing as the *Ironsides* made the bend and headed toward Lake Michigan. Indeed he had confidence in the Engelmann's boat. In fact he may have had more confidence in the boat than her own crew.

George Cowen was in his room napping as the *Ironsides* left Milwaukee. His shift began at one o'clock in the morning and he needed all of the rest that he could get. Shortly before the beginning of his watch, Cowen awoke to the feel of the *Ironsides* casually rolling in the seas. It was the familiar and comforting feeling of the boat being underway. As Cowen made his way into the engine room the heat of the boilers met his face while the smell of the coal and oil that made the boat come alive suddenly surrounded him. The engine room on a wooden steamer was a hard place to earn a living. Although the *Ironsides*' two steam engines were given plenty of room, this part of the boat was heavily enclosed with thick wooden walls and contained all of the heat from the steam plant. Temperatures normally hovered over the one hundred degree mark and there was precious little ventilation. In the daytime the engine room was illuminated by a huge skylight on the deckhouse roof, but at night there were only a few oil lamps to provide light. It was a hot, steamy, smelly, dark and dangerous place to make a living, and that was exactly the way fellows such as Cowen liked it. No sooner had Cowen entered the engine room than Chief McGlue came over and met him.

"Keep a close eye on the engine George," he ordered. "I'm goin' up to get some lunch."

Cowen nodded as the chief headed up the companionway. The engine of the *Ironsides* received as little investment from the Engelmanns as the rest of the boat, but the constant attention given it by the engineers kept it running like a fine pocket watch. Nearly an hour passed before Chief McGlue returned from his meal. Cowen dutifully reported that everything was running smoothly. McGlue took a fatherly scan around the engine. He listened to it working, he felt the deck beneath his feet and the vibration of the *Ironsides* and he decided that Cowen was right, everything was working fine. Once again he left the engine room in Cowen's charge and retired to his cabin for the night.

For the next 90 minutes the wooden deck beneath Cowen's feet rolled along in a normal manner. Then at half past three in the morning he felt the boat take on a nasty roll. The winds had turned from the southwest to the northwest and were beginning to blow a stiff gale. To the engine room crew, the weather outside was of little concern. Oilers Dan Hines, John Gilbert and Charles Wilcox spent their respective shifts moving around the steam engine and checking the assorted moving parts by placing an experienced hand upon the part. If the part felt too warm they would apply a dose of oil. This may sound like a trivial task, but without the constant attention of the oilers the engine of a steamer such as the *Ironsides* would grind itself to death in just a few hours. Down in the firehold the rest of engine room crew, the firemen, stoked the furnaces that heated the boat's boilers. Harry Hughes, Edward Fugle and James Brown shared that duty aboard the *Ironsides*. To all of these men their world aboard the *Ironsides* consisted largely of the engine room, their cabins and the galley. Occasionally one of them would sip a cup of coffee while leaning out the companionway and watching the lake go by, but most of their time was spent in the engine room. Actually, it did not matter if it was raining or snowing outside, the engine room never changed. It was always hot and dark and the job of keeping the boat running remained the same.

For engineers such as Cowen, there was another side to their job. Onboard a vessel the engineers are also the boat's handymen. The maintenance of every moving part of the *Ironsides*, from engine components to door hinges on passenger cabins, was their responsibility. Captain Sweetman placed his full trust in his engineers and when something went wrong, he expected them to simply fix it. If a small problem was beginning to grow into a large problem that may go beyond the scope of the engineers abilities, the captain expected to be informed. When you mix that sort of trust with the complacency of a person such as George Cowen and add in the tendency of the *Ironsides* to leak, you have a disastrous formula.

Shortly after the winds had shifted, the *Ironsides* began to corkscrew and roll in the following seas. As she rolled her hull stretched and twisted and those countless little leaks in her bottom began to let Lake Michigan in at an alarming rate. Soon water was sloshing up through the floor grating in the engine room. Upon inspection, Cowen scoffed with a "There she goes leakin' again," attitude. Remarkably, for the next hour and a half, the water continued to intrude while Cowen shrugged off the danger. After all, the boat had taken water on nearly every passage this season, so why should tonight be any different. Finally at five o'clock in the morning, the flooding got to the point where it annoyed Cowen and he used the bilge injection pump to force it out. In spite of this token effort, the flooding grew worse. At seven o'clock in the morning, three and one half hours after the flooding had started, the water in the bottom of the *Ironsides* had risen to the point where it was knee deep in the firehold and threatening to put out the boat's fires. The vessel had wallowed so low in the lake that the gangway doors on her sides were now vulnerable to the waves. In rapid succession the waves smashed in several of the thick wooden doors and Lake Michigan cascaded into the boat. As the waterfall of intruding doom came down the companionway stairs and burst into the engine room, Cowen decided it was time to send someone up to wake up the chief.

We can only imagine the thoughts that went through Chief McGlue's mind as he hustled down into his engine room and found it flooded with huge waves of filthy water sloshing from side to side as the *Ironsides* rolled. Cowen and other members of the engine room crew were frantically working the pumps in a pointless effort. One quick glance told McGlue all that he needed to know, the *Ironsides* was doomed. Minutes later the Chief was up in the pilothouse where Captain Sweetman was desperately trying to turn the boat around and put her head to the wind. The *Ironsides*, however, was hung up in the tough of the seas and not able to come around. Chief McGlue told the captain that he would go back down into the engine room and try backing one engine while running the other forward in the hope of pulling the boat out of the sea trough.

Down in the cargo hold, Tim Foley was working with his shipmates in a desperate battle to keep the lake out. They were using hand pumps to expel the water, but each wave brought in a hundred times more water than they could pump out. Shortly before nine o'clock the captain came down and mustered Tim and another crewman to help him raise the *Ironsides*' sail. He calculated that it would give them a couple of miles per hour toward the Grand Haven shore. Once the sail was up Captain Sweetman ordered Foley up to the pilothouse to "try to keep her in trim" with the wheel. Just then there was the sound of a volcano rumble and from every doorway that lead to the lower parts of the boat huge billows of steam erupted. Moments later there was shouting as the men of the engine crew came scrambling up. The water had put the boat's fires out and now she was powerless. Foley stopped on his way to the pilothouse and took off his new boots. He figured he was in for some swimming and they would only weigh him down.

"There goes seven dollars." He said as he tossed the new boots overboard.

Then he reached into his pocket and pulled out his knife. Using the knife he cut both of his pants legs off at the knees to make for easier swimming, then he headed up to the pilothouse. The wind was not gusting, but was instead blowing in a constant howl. In the confines of the bird cage pilothouse of the *Ironsides*, Tim Foley found it hard to maintain any sense of safety. It was clear to him that the boat was going down and the only real question was when she would take her dive. The seas were later described by acting Purser Norman Watkins as being "Two blocks wide at the base and in order to see the crests you had to look up at an angle of 70 degrees." You do not have to be good at math to figure out that this is a wild exaggeration. If you sit down and actually draw it out, using a common city block being 100 yards or 300 feet long, multiply that by two and then project a 70 degree angle from each end of that 600 foot base, they meet at a wave crest of just over 780 feet tall. That is about 20 times taller than the largest waves ever found on Lake Michigan. Considering the time of the year, and the normal weather patterns it is likely that the *Ironsides* was laboring in seas that were 12 to 18 feet at their worst. To Tim Foley it all made little difference. He was sure that he could outwit Lake Michigan. For that reason he took the boat's wheel and held it as steady as he could, just as Captain Sweetman had ordered.

Some witnesses ashore initially claimed that the *Ironsides* had attempted an approach to the harbor, but then turned back out into the lake. From the recorded accounts of the crew of the vessel, it appears that the *Ironsides* never was able to make such a maneuver. It is likely that what the witnesses ashore saw was the boat being spun about into the sea trough and they interpreted that as a turn. Although Foley held the vessel's wheel until she sank, he really had no effect on her course. There was no water passing over the rudder and so his hands on the wheel did nothing more than obey Captain Sweetman's orders.

Once the fires were out and the boilers could no longer make steam, the *Ironsides* was flooded to the point where waves were freely boarding through her smashed gangways. Only then was the decision made to alert the passengers. As Purser Watkins went around pounding his fist on each stateroom door the occupants were already well aware that they were on a sinking ship. Still, Watkins dutifully went to each cabin and told everyone to go to the lifeboats. Unlike most passenger vessels of this era, the *Ironsides* carried more than enough lifeboats for everyone onboard and so there would be no trouble in deciding who would go or who would stay. No such thing as a "lifeboat drill" was required or conducted aboard vessels of this era, however, and so there were no assigned lifeboat stations or procedures. Everyone was simply expected to find a boat with enough room left in it and get aboard. Then hope that the sailors manning the boat actually knew how to operate the rig.

Lifeboats from the *Ironsides* were lowered into the water first and then released from the davits. Passengers were loaded at the gangways and each boat was placed in the charge of a crew member. The first boat to be loaded was placed under the command of Henry Hazelbarth who was the first mate on the steamer *City Of Toledo*. That vessel was currently operating in the Engelmann fleet and he was on his way to meet her and sail her back to Milwaukee. He had made the dreadful mistake of bringing his wife along on this trip, the result being that now he was helping her into a lifeboat. After Mrs. Hazelbarth was safely seated, the little Valentine Boy was handed into her outstretched arms and seated. His mother followed and then both ladies hovered together to shelter the little boy. No one kept track of the number of passengers and crew who boarded this boat, but Sam Watkins, kin to the *Ironsides*' purser got in last and the lifeboat shoved off. At that same moment two

Lifeboats depart the floundering Ironsides. *Author's Collection.*

other lifeboats were being loaded. One of the boats was in the charge of Purser Norm Watkins and contained nine passengers. The other boat was placed in the charge of the ship's porter, Peter Riley and contained the ship's chamber maid, Maggie Young and eight passengers. Both of these boats got away from the *Ironsides* at about the same time and headed for shore. The fourth lifeboat was placed in the charge of Second Mate A.B. Pitman. A gaggle of crew, including Second Engineer Cowen, clamored aboard and the boat shoved off.

While Cowen's boat moved away from the *Ironsides*, the big steamer began rapidly sinking. They looked back and saw that First Mate Crosson had climbed the rigging of the foremast and was waving farewells toward the departing lifeboats. In a moment the whole wreck lurched and sank beneath him. The mast on which he had roosted snapped above him and swung down swatting him from the rigging like a golf club. Amazingly the steamer's hurricane deck remained on the surface. It is likely that this deck had broken away from the lower hull and was now left floating. This was fortunate for Cowen and the rest of the crew in his boat, because shortly after they departed the sinking *Ironsides*, their lifeboat capsized. They lost most of their oars and when they righted the lifeboat they had nothing to use to bail her out. Swimming as best they could, the crew of this lifeboat managed to drag it back to the wreck. Now the hurricane deck provided a temporary island upon which timid feet with soggy socks splashed about as the castaways went seeking provisions. They managed to scavenge some oars and a few buckets with which to bail and then returned to their lifeboat. Quickly she was rid of most of the water as they rowed away from the wreck. The men stopped long enough to pluck a battered Crosson from the lake and pull him to safety.

The last lifeboat to leave the *Ironsides* contained Captain Sweetman, Chief McGlue and Tim Foley. In all, five lifeboats and all of the passengers and crew were able to get away from the sinking *Ironsides*. Now they had a dangerous four mile journey to escape Lake Michigan. Second Engineer Cowen and his fellow castaways managed to fully free their lifeboat of some of its water and slid smoothly into Grand Haven harbor. There was a total of 16 people aboard that boat, but after it had been capsized and then re-righted they had all been dunked in Lake Michigan. Reportedly, seven of those on this lifeboat subsequently died of exposure on the way into the harbor. On a nearby beach north of Grand Haven the bow of the lifeboat under the care of ship's porter Peter Riley skidded into the sand as a breaking wave slammed into its stern. He had lost two occupants overboard on the way in. Charles Wimmel, who was a passenger, was washed out by a wave and consumed by Lake Michigan. One of the ship's cooks, whose name is recorded as both "Dundasher" and "Dundas" was also washed from the lifeboat. He managed to swim over a mile to shore and survived. The lifeboat that was being managed by Purser Watkins got to within a half mile of the beach when Lake Michigan reached out and flipped it over. Everyone in the boat was flung into the water, yet all of them made it back to the lifeboat. They all clung to their turtled lifeboat until they were washed ashore and pulled from the lake by local residents.

Ed Killian, who ran the "Milwaukee House" in Grand Haven immediately opened his doors to the survivors. In fact the entire town of Grand Haven came to the aid of the castaways. Hundreds of people lined the beaches and the men in town who were the strongest swimmers were poised to dive into the surf and recover both the living and the dead. Unfortunately, after Norman Watkins' overturned lifeboat and the nine people who were clinging to it were dragged to safety, all that remained for the swimmers to recover were dead bodies. Somewhere between the wreck and the beach, Captain Sweetman's lifeboat had been overturned by Lake Michigan and all aboard it were drown. That toll included Tim Foley whose youthful self image of being able to escape, no matter what the lake tried to do to him, had proven to be terribly wrong. Also capsized by the lake was the lifeboat under the command of Henry Hazelbarth. As the first mate on the *City Of Toledo*, he was considered to be an extremely competent sailor and well able to handle the lifeboat under any circumstances. Still, Lake Michigan got the better of him and tossed his lifeboat over, dumping its human cargo into the icy water. Out of all of those who occupied the lifeboat, only Sam Watkins managed to swim the one and one half mile distance to shore. This was his second brush with Lake Michigan in just three months. He had been out on the lake on the sloop *Lake Breeze* on the fourth of July when a powerful squall came past. The boat was turtled and Sam had to cling to its overturned hull and wait until another vessel came by and rescued him and the other man who had been aboard. Now he had survived a second attempt by Lake Michigan to take his life.

Through the day the lake continued to deposit bodies onto the beach north of Grand Haven. During that time the body of Mrs. Valentine was pulled from the surf by local residents and after some searching of the beach the body of her five year old son, dressed in his blue sailor's suit, was found half buried in the sand. A day later a dozen of the bodies from the *Ironsides* were returned to Milwaukee in plain pine boxes aboard the Engelmann steamer *Saginaw*. In a scene of sorrow the next of kin met the boxes at the Engelmann's dock and warehouse. Nearby sat the damaged cargo that had been wetted in the *Ironsides*' previous trip. Henry Valentine came to identify and claim his wife and little boy. Looking at the little sailor the grieving father wondered "Why?"

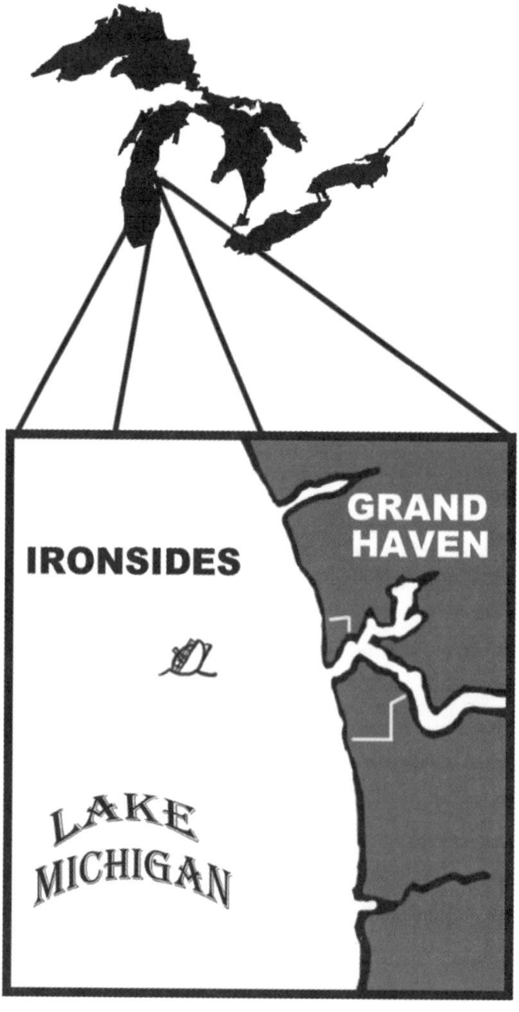

Survivors who worked for Engelmann Transportation gave self-serving statements to the press wherein they flatly denied that the *Ironsides* had ever leaked. The most unconvincing of these came from Second Engineer Cowen who denied that the boat had ever leaked, but later stated that the water was coming in "from the bottom" of the boat. Such statements make sense when you consider that when the *Ironsides* went down, these folks were suddenly all unemployed. There would be little hope that Engelmann Transportation would hire them back if they had told the press that the *Ironsides* was a leaking tub.

Of course a blue ribbon panel of vessel owners and local politicians was assembled in Grand Haven to investigate the sinking of the *Ironsides*. Although other steamers of the same size, construction and age were out on Lake Michigan in that same weather, and all of them got into their docks without wetting one piece of their cargo, the investigators said that there was no evidence to show that the *Ironsides* was in a leaking or otherwise unseaworthy condition. The wet cargoes that remained on the docks at both Grand Haven and Milwaukee were advantageously overlooked and the accounts of those who thought they had witnessed the *Ironsides* make a turn away from Grand Haven were considered instead. The blame was put onto Captain Sweetman for turning his boat away from a safe port and heading her into the storm where the waves then pounded her until she sank. The fact that the surviving engineer had stated that Chief McGlue reversed one engine and went forward on the other, but they still could not get the boat to turn from the sea trough was also overlooked. Since both Captain Sweetman and Chief McGlue were dead, it was somewhat hard for them to testify. So it was that the captain of the *Ironsides* was blamed for the sinking because he was said to have made a turn that he could never have preformed. The Engelmanns were, naturally, cleared of all blame by their peers.

All of the deaths in this wreck were caused by the lifeboats over turning and dumping their passengers into the lake. Upon a closer investigation done without the influence of those long dead robber barons and politicians of the *Ironsides*' era, we can conclude that the situation by which all of the people were killed may have actually been caused by the addition of safety equipment rather than a lack of safety equipment. When the *Ironsides* was built, she was equipped with eight lifeboats.

Each lifeboat was designed to accommodate more than 20 people. This meant that the weight of that many bodies was calculated into the stability of each lifeboat. The mass of those 20 plus people was needed to ballast the lifeboats. With less than ten people in a given lifeboat, that boat would ride high in the water, would be unstable and would then be easily capsized in the waves. Only two of the five lifeboats that were launched from the *Ironsides* reached shore upright. One was the boat guided by the ship's porter which had 13 people aboard and the other was the boat that had been capsized and re-righted. That boat had sixteen people aboard and since we can assume that they did not get all of the water out of it after it was capsized, it probably had a foot of water in the bottom which acted as additional ballast. It managed to remain upright and travel more than four miles without being flipped over. The boats that were capsized the farthest distance from shore, being Captain Sweetman's boat and the boat commanded by Henry Hazelbarth, each had less than five people aboard. The remaining lifeboat, which was also capsized, had eight people aboard. Considering this information, we can conclude that the people aboard the *Ironsides* would have been better off if she had carried just two lifeboats rather than eight. The loss of life would have been greatly reduced if everyone had been forced to squeezed into two lifeboats, and thereby ballasted and stabilized those boats, rather than dividing the population among five lifeboats which were then in an unstable condition. So it may have been that the excess of lifeboats on the *Ironsides*, that brought so much comfort to her passengers, contributed to the great loss of life in the boat's sinking.

Without doubt, in the years that followed the loss of the *Ironsides*, each time that Henry Valentine looked out across Lake Michigan he envisioned his wife and son. He felt the pain of their loss and wondered about their last minutes on the lake. We too can look toward the lake and wonder about that little boy in the sailor's suit bobbing in the huge waves after being thrown from the *Ironsides*' lifeboat. How many times did his little voice call out for "Help!" and is it still being heard today. Was the voice that was heard aboard the *Mackinaw* in the fog that day in the year 2000 the ghost of that little boy calling out from across the years? If they had found the place from where the voice in the fog originated would they have found the ghost of the *Ironsides* and the lost little boy in a blue sailor's suit?

Midnight And *Mears*

For nearly a century the business of sailing ships and lumber hookers has been absent from the shores of the lower Great Lakes. On Lake Huron, places such as Alpena ,Tawas, and Oscoda have nearly forgotten the ships that once dotted the horizon. Likewise, the sawmills and lumber docks that studded the shoreline have faded into history and have been replaced by marinas, condominium complexes and plush beach houses. Still the ghosts of the days of "king lumber" are never far below the surface. In fact, on occasion, the sands wash back and Lake Huron sends its waves to reveal the bones of one of her long forgotten victims. The remains of a once proud ship that had fallen prey to the lake's temper suddenly appear in the shallow water near the shore or even in the dunes of the beach itself. Oddly, the lake's showing of its prize is usually overlooked or mistaken for being "Just an old dock." Too often the story that surrounds the wreck has been forgotten. In other cases, the bones of the wreck reach out across time and touch the lives of those who walk the beaches. Artifacts, if considered closely, can tell the story of a long forgotten disaster. Amazingly all of this often lays just below the feet of frolicking vacationers or strolling beach house owners.

From his tiny two seat peddle-powered paddleboat, Dr. John O'Shea was navigating the waters of Lake Huron with his son Brennan on a pleasant August afternoon in the summer of 1998. Originally he had aboard a crew of two, but his other son, Cailen, had recently jumped ship in order to swim in the shallow waters and play in the waves. This entire scene was taking place on the south side of Au Sable Point, a jut of land that is located just below Oscoda, Michigan. Au Sable Point, once known as "Fish Point" is today fringed with posh homes and summer cottages. A carpet of fine beach sand leads to the lake and is jealously guarded by the local residents. It is a wonderful place to vacation and a better place to live. The O'Shea family had recently built a nice cabin on the point and this visit was their first chance to really enjoy their new family resort without the commotion of new construction.

By the time that Dr. O'Shea turned his attention from the operation of his paddleboat, back toward the beach, Cailen was no longer swimming but was now walking along the beach. In his hand, he carried a strange looking wooden object and every few steps along the beach he would stop and hammer the ground with it. With a watchfulness that only a father can muster, the senior O'Shea kept track of his beachcombing son. Finally he simply had to find out what the boy was carrying. Setting the paddleboat ashore, he hiked his way along the beach and intercepted his son. The object in Cailen's possession was a strange looking mallet. Dr. O'Shea, a professor of anthropology at the University of Michigan, had never seen anything like it. The mallet's wooden head was unusually large, about 18 inches long, and had wide metal bands. The handle of the tool was about two feet long and was attached to the head with two brass rivets that had been weathered green. In a heartbeat, Dr. O'Shea's skilled anthropologist's eye recognized this as an historic artifact. In fact it was the type of object that really turns on the buttons of someone with his training. He immediately began to question Cailen as to where he had found the mallet. The boy explained that he was swimming in the shallows and had found the mallet just sitting on the bottom in about three feet of water. He had decided to stop swimming in the area because there were too many metal spikes sticking up and they were hurting his feet. With the mallet in hand Dr. O'Shea gazed back toward the lake and the area that Cailen had indicated. For a long moment he pondered the facts. Odd wooden tools, metal spikes on the lake bottom. Suddenly, the beach and water, whose beauty and tranquility had charmed him into building a vacation cottage in this area, took on a new and far more complex appearance.

Being a professional anthropologist, Dr. O'Shea knew instantly that the artifact in his hands needed to be preserved, and so he went to work. First, the artifact needed to be stabilized, and that meant placing it back into the same type of environment from which Cailen had removed it. Using a wet towel, the mallet was carefully wrapped and thus protected from the surrounding air in the same manner as the sands at the bottom of the lake had protected it. Next, the artifact needed to be evaluated and identified. For that, Dr. O'Shea turned to Dr. John Halsey, Archaeologist for the State of Michigan. In the days that followed the discovery, Dr. O'Shea contacted the office of the State Archaeologist. Dr. Halsey

Scarf-cut beam from either the Midnight *or* Mears. *Author's Collection.*

knew both Dr. O'Shea and his reputation as an anthropologist and agreed to come to Au Sable Point and inspect the mallet. He immediately identified the artifact as being a ship's caulking mallet. This tool was used to pound caulk into the cracks between the timbers of a wooden vessel and keep them from leaking. During his visit, the State Archaeologist also took the time to wade out into the area where Cailen had reported the metal spikes. Dr. O'Shea could recall the local folks talking in nebulous terms about old shipwrecks in the area, but not being a shipwreck scholar himself, O'Shea had never given much consideration to the subject. What Halsey found would alter Dr. O'Shea's perceptions of Great Lakes shipwrecks as well as the waters near his cottage. There, in the shallow water were large pieces of a wooden vessel. In later scuba dives, Halsey found additional pieces of wreckage scattered around on the bottom. The following year, the waves uncovered a huge wooden ship's keel that rested in the surf like the bones of a dinosaur. Soon the questions about the wreck hung over O'Shea's shoulders like a ghost waiting for him to uncover the story of its passing. Now those waves, whose rhythm so pleasantly sounded through the windows of the O'Shea cottage before the mallet's discovery, took on a different tone. They seemed to remind the anthropologist that somewhere out there, buried in the sands outside of his window, was the physical evidence of how the old mariners lived and worked. They called to him, "It's all waiting, come and find it."

November of 1889 was about to expire as Captain Frank Ocha, the keeper of the Ottawa Point Lifesaving Station, surveyed Lake Huron. Ottawa Point, which in modern times is known as Tawas Point is located about ten miles south of Au Sable Point and the Ottawa Point Lifesaving Station was one of the original 1876 establishments. Being on the north side of the point, the station normally had its boathouse doors in the face of November's gales and today was no exception. The

Broken keel of the Mears. *Author's photo.*

wind was screaming from nearly due north and building a frightful surf. So strong were the gusts of wind that they were ripping the crests from the towering seas and slinging the spray directly at the station's windows where it was instantly freezing into a rapidly thickening sheet of ice. As an added bonus, the gale was spitting thick snow in an opaque blizzard that obscured the lake beyond. As he listened to the wind howl through the cracks in the boathouse doors he considered that if the crew were called upon to launch their surfboat, they would never be able to breech the breaking waves. He also reckoned that although, per regulation, he had one of the surfmen atop the station's roof in the watch tower, it was a pointless duty. There was no way in a blizzard such as this that the surfman on watch could see beyond a few feet onto the lake. Still, if there was any sort of weather that would produce the worst sort of shipwreck, this was it. For that reason Keeper Ocha had ordered that a fresh pot of hot coffee be kept on the stove along side a hot kettle of soup. If the call came, and the boys had to launch, they would all go out with hot food and coffee in their bellies–they would need it. The unofficial motto of the lifesaving service kept going through his mind, "You have to go out, but you don't have to come back." It was the 27th day of November and in just three days the lifesaving station would be closed for the season. The day prior to that would be National Thanksgiving and Ocha was planning a fair feast at his station to reward the crew for their hard work and attention to duty through the past season. Before that, however, Keeper Ocha knew that they would have to see this gale through. If the call came, they all had to go out, but they did not have to come back ...alive.

Flipping open his pocket watch, Keeper Ocha noted that the hands read just beyond half past two o'clock in the afternoon. The gale had been blowing since just before sunrise and showed no sign of letting up. Each gust of wind seemed to shake the wood frame of the station as snow occasionally found its way inside through unseen gaps in the woodwork. Ocha could see that the storm was beginning to grow stronger. What he could not see was the scene two dozen miles north, obscured by the blizzard. What was happening north of Au Sable Point at that moment would cause his men to be called to "go out" and do their duty.

Above Au Sable Point, groping in a shroud of blowing white snow, was the 185 foot long lumber steamer *Wilhelm.* Following behind her attached to thick towing hawsers came the schooner-barges *Mears* and *Midnight.* All three vessels were downbound for Buffalo, New York and loaded with stacks of lumber. To say that they were taking a bad dusting from the gale would be an understatement. In fact the *Wilhelm* was able to make just about eight miles per hour in her loaded condition and with two deeply laden schooner-barges attached to her heels her speed was reduced even more. On their heels the little flotilla had a north wind blowing at a speed of nearly ten times their own speed. This wind was driving waves that towered nearly 20 feet tall and was smashing them against the stern quarters of the three boats. From the *Wilhelm's* pilothouse it was impossible to see either of the two consorts, all that the steamer's people could see was the towing hawser as it stretched into the blizzard and sheered from one side to the next as the winds set upon the schooner-barges. The view had been the same all day.

As darkness began to set in, the *Wilhelm's* captain was still navigating by compass, sounding lead, instinct and luck. He knew that he had the three vessels somewhere near Tawas Bay and if he could keep the tow together and squeak in close enough to Ottawa Point, he may see the lighthouse through the blizzard and be able to run into the sheltered bay to wait the storm out. The steamer's sounding lead was good, the compass was accurate and the captain's instincts were sharp, but the luck ran out at four o'clock that evening. It was then that the towing hawser suddenly went slack and the *Wilhelm* could be felt to surge ahead. Her schooner-barges had broken loose and were now adrift out in the gale. Dutifully, the *Wilhelm* came around in an effort to locate and recover her barges. But groping in huge seas and blinded by the blizzard, there was no way that the steamer's crew could ever find the wayward schooner-barges. The evening was rapidly turning ink-black and the barges were marked only by dim oil lamps in their running lights. Odds are that the waves had probably snuffed the lamps out long before the *Wilhelm* needed them anyway. The only choice for the steamer now was to run for Tawas Bay, alert the lifesavers, and hope that the barges could ride out the gale on their own until help arrived.

At five o'clock that evening, Keeper Ocha was about to exchange his lookout man for the nightly beach patrol when the lookout came bounding down the stairs saying that a steamer was blowing distress signals over on the bay. The life-savers always kept the station sloop tied up on the bay side of the point as it was the easiest way to get to the town of East Tawas. The road down the point was little more than a trail through nearly four miles of thick woods and swamp. Thus the best way to get into town was to simply sail across the bay. Leaving his number one surfman in charge, Keeper Ocha headed out to the vessel that was blowing the distress signals. As he pulled up along side the battered *Wilhelm*, Ocha saw her crew busy at trying to re-trim what was left of her deck load of lumber. From over the steamer's rail her captain shouted through the blizzard toward the squinting keeper and told him of the two barges that had broken loose above Au Sable. Keeper Ocha got the message and immediately headed across the bay toward East Tawas. He intended to telegraph Au Sable and learn the condition of the barges. Unfortunately, in a bad storm such as that one, the very first victims were usually the telegraph lines. Indeed the fragile lines were down somewhere between East Tawas and Au Sable and there was no way to communicate up the coast. Keeper Ocha would have to devise a new plan.

Returning to the lifesaving station at eight o'clock that evening, Keeper Ocha mustered his surfmen. Although Au Sable Point is only five and one half miles rowing distance from the lifesaving station, the winds and seas made it impossible for the storm warriors to attempt that trek by water. Additionally, the storm had cast so much driftwood and other debris onto the beach that passage that way was also blocked. Ocha's crew would have to go the distance by way of the inland trail, also known as "the sand trail." The distance by way of the sand trail from the station to Au Sable was just over 12 miles. Keeper Ocha was not one to lose his head and go running off on a wild goose chase. There was the very real probability that the two schooner-barges had found safe anchorage and were now safely riding the storm out at the ends of their chains. His duty was to keep a watch over the waters surrounding his station and there were many other vessels out on the lake that could find themselves in danger in his area of responsibility. If he and his crew were off a dozen miles north on a false alarm when some other boat had a real wreck closer to his station, he would be responsible for the loss of life. Frank Ocha was one of a lifesaving family. His brother, Albert Ocha, was currently the keeper of the Ship Canal station up on Lake Superior. Albert was famed for an amazing effort of, on two different occasions, traveling a distance of 110 miles by train to rescue the crews of vessels off of Marquette. So it was that when Keeper Frank Ocha may have had it in his blood to keep cool and plan well. Before committing his crew to a 12 mile hike, he had to know for sure if the boats at Au Sable were in real danger. Thus he came up with a sound course of action. Surfmen Gill and Carpenter were ordered to hike up to Au Sable and find out about the two vessels. As soon as they discovered something conclusive, one of them was to head back to the station and inform Ocha, the other was to proceed to the wreck site, build a bonfire and signal the crew aboard the wreck that help was on the way. Meanwhile, Keeper Ocha would still retain enough of his crew at the station to effect a rescue if another vessel should wreck in his area.

Even in modern times with a modern highway to lead the way, hiking to Au Sable Point would be a marathon. In 1889, with a blizzard and gale blowing, surfmen Gill and Carpenter found that the going was a shivering struggle. Once they had gotten off of Tawas Point and the trail turned to the north, the wind was funneled down through the trees and directly into their faces. The snow was blinding and each man was being stung by the blowing sleet as it pelted their eyes. To make the trek worse, branches and trees were being blown over as the surfmen passed. If this trip turned out to be a false alarm, the frostbitten surfmen would surely have earned their day's pay of $1.66.

Off of Au Sable Point, the crews of the *Midnight* and *Mears* were finding their situation to be far worse than that of the two surfmen. When the towline to the *Wilhelm* had broken,

Captain Hill of the *Midnight* and Captain Hazen of the *Mears* both knew immediately what had happened. The first roll of their boats said that they were adrift. Neither master knew quite where they were. The blizzard had obscured every landmark and both boats may as well have had a giant white sheet tossed over them. Still, the procedure for saving ones boat in this case was fairly simple. Clear away the anchors and drop the hooks down to catch Lake Huron's sandy bottom, let your boat come head to the winds and ride out the gale. Dropping the huge anchors on a schooner-barge was no easy task, however. Each anchor could weigh more than a ton, and the rig had to be hoisted by hand, then swung over the rail and released. Each vessel had just four men to accomplish this task and the chore would take time. It was time that Lake Huron refused to grant the two vessels.

No sooner had the task of dropping the anchors been started than the gale blew the *Midnight* and *Mears* aground. Heavily loaded with lumber, the hulls of the two schooner-barges found the bottom of the lake less than 100 yards off of Au Sable Point. It is not recorded which of the two lakers was in the lead, but no sooner had one found the bottom than the other was smashed beam to beam with her fleet mate. Now held together rail-to-rail by the wind, the two boats were shoved by the seas across the tip of Au Sable Point. Groaning in the sand and with 18 foot waves of ice water exploding over them, plucking away the huge boards of their lumber cargo, Lake Huron played with its prey like a cat with two wounded mice. Spinning around as if on ice the vessels were boarded by every wave. Among the first items stripped away from each boat by Huron's bitter cold claws were their lifeboats. Mounted athwartwise across their sterns the hanging lifeboats were an easy target for the lake. Now, no matter what else the lake had in store for the *Midnight* and *Mears*, it had assured that their crews were trapped aboard. South, along Au Sable Point the vessels were pushed, right past the place where modern property owners today bask on beautiful sandy beaches. Finally, 200 yards to the lee side of the point, the *Midnight* and *Mears* came to rest, side by side with their bows pointed to the north.

Believing that the *Mears* was the stronger of the two boats, the crew of the *Midnight* wasted no time in abandoning their boat and jumping to the deck of Captain Hazen's command. Convinced that he would soon be in for a long swim, Daniel Mowat quickly began stripping off his oilskin storm clothing. The hearty Scottish sailor thought he was well able to take the drenching of the lake and stroke his way to the beach if the boat beneath him suddenly decided to come apart. Having often swung the mallet to caulk the hulls of wooden lakers, he had spent many a night pondering the subject of shipwrecks and if a boat was going to go to pieces beneath his feet, he did not want the heavy oilskins weighing him down. Lake Huron, however, was not about to be so quick with the *Midnight* and *Mears* or their crews.

While Mowat prepared for the *Mears* to break up, everyone else seemed to move in slow motion. Then a huge wave broke solidly over the wrecks. That wave grabbed any item handy and carried it down upon the survivors. Having just set foot upon the *Mears*, Elijah Powers, the *Midnight's* mate glanced toward the rumbling wave and to his horror saw a huge water cask rolling toward him like a freight train. Instinctively, Powers put his arm up as if to shield himself just before the cask ran him over. Washed along the deck like a rag doll, he clawed at any fixture to stop his motion in the frigid water and managed to hold on to something until the wave expended itself. Moments later he attempted to get to his feet, but found intense pain. The cask had hit him like a runaway horse cart and left him with a broken leg. As each wave broke over the wrecks they caused equal havoc and it was immediately clear that if the people were to survive, they would have to shelter in the fo'c'sle of the *Mears*. As all twelve castaways gathered in the tiny space in the wooden bow of the *Mears*, the captain's took a head count. No one was missing, but the situation was not good. Mowat had lost all of his protective clothing and was now soaked and shivering. Powers was suffering from his broken leg. Worst of all, the temperature was below freezing and there was no heat and no way to produce any sort of a fire. Outside, Lake Huron's waves thundered against the timbers of the Mears' hull as the night grew dark. No one knew if their wrecks had been discovered or if they would ever be discovered. There was no way to know if help was on the way or if they would simply perish from the cold, one by one. Outside there was nothing but the raging lake and the shore lined with trees. The two boats could go to pieces within 200 yards of land and in this isolated spot, no one would ever know. It was a cold, wet and hopeless situation for the crews of the *Midnight* and *Mears*.

After three hours, the two surfmen from the Ottawa Point Life Saving station had made a distance of nine miles toward Au Sable and they were nearly exhausted. That was when they came upon the house of the Spencer brothers and decided to impose upon them for a bit of shelter and warmth before proceeding on. The stay for the two storm warriors, however, was brief. No sooner had they been invited into the house than the Spencers informed them that two vessels had indeed wrecked on Au Sable Point. It was this news that got the blood of the two storm warriors pumping in a way that no cup of stimulants could. Suddenly, their numb toes and frostbitten faces were forgotten. Surfman Gill set out dashing back to the station to alert the rest of the crew. Meanwhile, one of the Spencer brothers agreed to guide Carpenter to the site of the wrecks.

At a moment such as this, a lifesaver does not think of his meager earnings, or the endless nights of boredom spent walking beach patrol. Gill's feet had wings as he ran along the path that he and Carpenter had previously struggled to hike upon. In the darkness with only a dim oil burning patrol lantern to light the way, he hurtled fallen trees and kicked through snow drifts as he was propelled by pure adrenaline.

Meanwhile, Carpenter reached the site that Spencer indicated. It was the point on the shore that he thought was closest to the wrecks and although the wrecks could not be seen in the distance, Spencer insisted that they were out there. Carpenter reached into his belt and got a Coston signal. These handheld signals were similar to modern road flares. Taking the three inch long Coston cartridge from the pouch, he fit it into the top of his wooden Coston handle. Then he held the handle near the opposite end with one hand an using the palm of his other hand

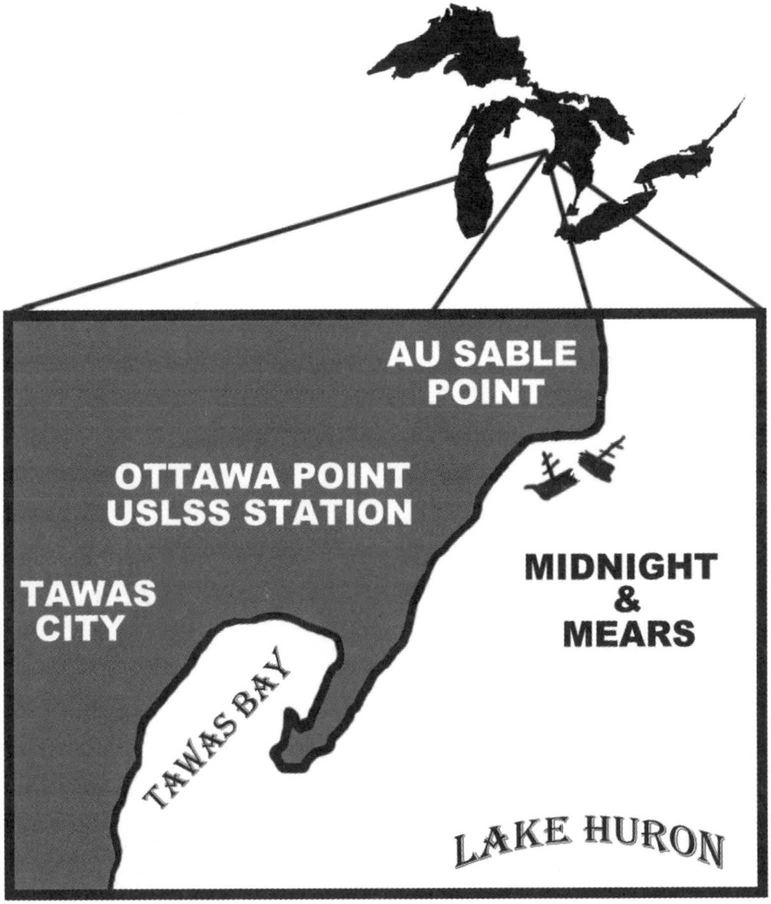

he smacked the plunger at the bottom of the handle. Spencer took a step back as the device began to make a loud sizzling sound, and then a brilliant pinkish red light seemed to glow in every direction. Held overhead a Coston signal could be seen for as far as 20 miles offshore. Their bright flame could even penetrate fog and blizzards to a degree. Waving the burning flare over his head, surfman Carpenter signaled into the blackness as his station keeper had ordered. This stormy night was so dark that there was no way that Carpenter could see more than a few yards into the lake and the howling wind made shouting a communication a pointless effort. Still he waved the Coston toward the blackness of the distance in the hope that the wrecks were actually out there and that someone may be watching. For about two minutes the two men stood in the pink light of the illuminated blizzard on the wind swept beach as the signal slowly burned and then fizzled into darkness.

"Now what?" Spencer asked.

"We need to gather up as much of this driftwood as we can," Carpenter replied as he knocked the expended cartridge from his Coston handle "We're gonna build a big bon fire and keep it burning until daylight."

Gill's strength had just about run out by the time that he arrived back at the lifesaving station. In a near state of collapse he told Keeper Ocha that there were indeed shipwrecks on Au Sable Point. It was 1:40 in the morning when the exhausted, frost bitten surfman reached the station. He had made the distance between the Spencer home and the station in just over two hours, cutting nearly a full hour off of his and Carpenter's trip north. In all, Gill had traveled a distance of nearly 20 miles, on foot, in the dark, in knee-deep snow, in sub freezing temperatures, in a blizzard, in a time of five hours and 40 minutes.

Surfman Gill would have plenty of time to rest. That was because now that there had been confirmation of the wrecks, Keeper Ocha and his men needed to deploy to the scene, but there was only one way to get there and that was back along the same route that Gill had just traveled The waves were far too rough to make the distance by boat, so the surfmen would have to go by land. The beach was filled with huge chunks of driftwood, many pieces of which were complete trees, and was thus impassable. Considering such circumstance, the United States Life Saving Service had supplied all of its stations with two carts, one for the beach rescue equipment and another for the lifeboat. The service was, however, run on a shoestring budget and so the one element that was not supplied were the horses to pull the carts. In fact, the station's crew were expected to pull the carts in most cases. In the event that horses were needed, each station keeper was expected to go to the local town and make a deal with some local livery stable to have a standing account to rent horses when needed and have a team always on standby. This, of course, did not mean that the stable owners were ready and waiting 24 hours a day with a team hitched and ready to go just in case of a shipwreck. What it meant in this case was that Ocha had to send surfman Whitchurch through the woods to Tawas in the middle of the night to wake the teamster, rig the horses and then bring them back out onto Tawas Point to get the carts.

From the station to the town of East Tawas surfman Whitchurch would have to travel a distance of four miles and some of that was through swamp. Fortunately, one thing that the storm had done in the lifesavers favor was to freeze the swamp solid. Once in the sleeping town, the surfman went to the livery stable and beat on the door until teamster Donohue was awakened. By the time that the two men had four horses rigged and headed back to the station, it was near dawn.

Out on Au Sable Point, surfman Carpenter had spent all night keeping watch on the area of the wrecks. At times during the night he thought that he could hear shouts coming from out on the wrecks. On each of those occasions he answered by burning another Coston signal. The only reply to his signals would be the howling winds and the roaring of the surf. We can only imagine his feeling of helplessness. Here was a dedicated lifesaver, a man who had trained every day to rescue people from shipwrecks and now all he could do was stand and blindly wave Coston flares toward the darkness. It was not until the dawn began that he could finally make out the silhouettes of two large objects in the distance. As each minute of growing daylight passed the objects began to grow more clear as did Carpenter's alarm. Long before actual daylight fully illuminated the scene, the surfman could see the rolling seas breaking completely over the two sunken schooner-barges. Each wave seemed to drown the boats, and their hulks were encased in ice. Worse yet, the hulls appeared to be slithering in the waves and that meant that they were breaking up. The scene was more frightening than anything Carpenter had imagined. If anyone was still alive aboard the wrecks, they would not last much longer. Giving Spencer instructions to keep the bon fire alive and as large as possible, Carpenter headed off to find his fellow lifesavers and pass on the urgency of the situation.

Aboard the wrecked *Mears* the scene had long passed the point of terror and fear and had degraded into a numbing cold wait for death. Through the long black hours of the frigid night as the waves of ice water pounded, once every few seconds, against the hull of *Mears*, the dozen people huddled in the cramped wooden cave that was her fo'c'sle, had completely given up any thought of ever being warm again. It seemed as if they would be forever cold and sooner than later they would be dead. They had passed from the worry that the boat's timbers would break apart to the hope that the hull would crumble and the lake would take them and relieve their suffering. No one moved much anymore. It caused too much pain to move their frozen limbs. Daniel Mowat was the worst off of the group. Having shed his protective oil skins and then seeing them swept away by the lake, he had only his shirt sleeves and trousers to keep him warm. He had stopped shivering many hours before dawn and was now slipping in and out of consciousness. The cold daylight found them all huddled together, simply waiting to die.

Hauling the lifeboat and beach cart with the horses had been a slow task. Keeper Ocha had to send some of the surfmen ahead to clear the fallen trees and the wheels of the carts kept getting clogged with snow. Surfman Carpenter met his fellow lifesavers four miles from the wreck site and promptly informed Ocha that he thought the only way to get to the wrecks would be by use of the Lyle gun and breeches buoy. The surf, he reckoned, was far too rough to launch the boat. Hearing that Ocha left the boat and the crew continued on with just the beach cart. The compact two-wheeled cart was far easier for the horses to pull and now they made far better progress toward the wrecks.

Noon was the hour when the Ottawa Point lifesavers reached the wrecks. Keeper Ocha immediately saw that Carpenter's evaluation of the situation was correct, but he sent teamster Donohue back up the trail to get the abandoned surfboat anyhow. If the gun did not work, they would use the boat to make the rescue or die trying. Next his crew went about their planned and practiced step-by-step drill of preparing the Lyle gun and shot line. As the crew had practiced once a week through the entire season, the gun was rigged and fired. The line lodged squarely in the rigging of the *Mears* as the crowd of local folks, who were now gathered on the beach, cheered. The sound of the cannon-like Lyle gun going off had gotten the attention of the frozen castaways aboard the *Mears* and two crewmen came out from the shelter of the fo'c'sle to find the lifeline hanging from the rigging. With benumbed hands they started pulling on the line and hauled the whip line aboard. Then they went about rigging the block so that the breeches buoy could be sent out. As this process went on the waves and current tried to slack and tangle the line as the lifesavers wrestled with it. Helping hands from the crowd of local folks pitched in and kept the line taut. At that moment, the lifesavers and the residents of Au Sable Point all stood together and dug their feet into the sand to save the people of the *Midnight* and *Mears*.

Because of the ice that coated the wrecks, and the waves that swept their decks as well as the benumbed condition of the sailors, the best that they could do was to rig the tail block for the breeches buoy just a bit above deck level. This meant that whoever made the trip ashore in the rig would surely get a soaking as it went along. Immediately the breeches buoy was sent out and one of the two crewmen who had rigged the line got in it. As the lifesavers took the slack out of the rope and it came out of the lake, the air was so cold that it stiffened and froze. Still the people ashore pulled. Again, the hands of the Au Sable Point residents pulled with the hands of the lifesavers against Lake Huron. Still, they could not keep the line from slacking and the luckless sailor was dragged most of the way dunked in the ice water seas. When he was finally pulled onto dry land he was nearly insensible and it was not until he was taken close to the heat of the bonfire that he was able to speak.

When the survivor told of the situation aboard the *Mears* it became clear that a change of plan would be needed and not a second could be wasted. He told of how Mowat had died of the cold and how Mate Powers was suffering with a broken leg. The two ladies aboard, Captain Hazen's wife and Mary McDonald, were in frail condition and would surely not survive the soaking that he had just been through. Worst of all, the *Midnight* was rapidly breaking up and the *Mears* would soon follow.

Just as the castaway was telling his frozen story, teamster Donohue was coming onto the beach pulling the surfboat and cart. Again the local folks swarmed in to help and as the lifesavers got aboard, the eager crowd helped launch the lifeboat. For a moment Ocha thought that some of them may actually try to climb aboard. Instead they simply launched and bid the storm warriors good luck. Meeting each wave guided by skill and strengthened by courage, the crew of the Ottawa Point station bent at their oars as Lake Huron reached out to slap them with a November resentment. Then they handily moved over and took hold of the line that was attached to the wreck. Hand over hand the lifesavers hauled their boat out to the *Mears* with efficiency. Twice a week, in all sorts of weather these lifesavers had practiced with this boat. This was not a snow-choked trail in the back woods, it was not a swamp, it was instead the place where they were the most skilled. They had spent months practicing at beating Lake Huron and today she was no match for them.

Pulling up under the *Mears*, the storm warriors were just about to make the deck when Huron sent a rogue wave to sweep them from their grip on the line. With the rhythm of a well trained team they all went to their oars and pulled back into position. A grapnel hook was tossed over the wreck's rail and surfman Smith went aboard the *Mears*. He discovered a huddled gaggle of survivors who looked more dead than alive. All of the people had hair frozen white with ice and their clothing was frozen stiff upon them. One by one Smith coaxed each of the frozen souls to the rail and into the lifeboat. As this process went on there came a loud creaking sound like that of a toppling tree. It was the mizzen mast of the *Mears* as it came falling down. The boat's stern was also beginning to come apart as Lake Huron chewed at it. As Smith got the last survivor off he went back to get the body of Daniel Mowat, which was laying frozen to the deck, but the *Mears* would not wait. She began to go to pieces beneath Smith's boots and he had no choice other than getting away with his life.

Now Keeper Ocha turned his surfboat and headed for shore. Standing triumphantly at the tiller he guided the sleek rescue boat toward the beach as his crew pulled at their oars and the crowd cheered above the storm. Pulled onto dry land by the hands of the folks of Au Sable point the survivors of the *Midnight* and *Mears* were at last safe. Still, they were all in bad condition. Captain Hazen was delirious from the cold and the ladies were in shock. They were taken by sleigh to a local home a mile away and allowed to recover there.

Meanwhile, teamster Donohue rigged his horses and a cart and took two surfmen and all of the other survivors back toward the lifesaving station. About half way to the station the team of horses simply refused to pull any farther. They were exhausted and no amount of coaching from the teamster would make them move. Fortunately, they were near a farm house, so the lifesavers headed there to see if they could find some temporary shelter. It turned out that the residents were just sitting down to Thanksgiving dinner and had plenty of heat and food to share. In the United States Life Saving Service's Annual Report to Congress for the fiscal year of 1890, it is officially said of the event, "Few Thanksgiving dinners were ever eaten with greater thankfulness and relish than was this simple repast at that lonely farmhouse in the Michigan woods."

Later that same day Keeper Ocha returned to the wrecks to help recover the station's equipment. By that time the *Mears* had rolled on her side and was rapidly breaking up while the *Midnight* was almost gone. Donohue and his people got to the Ottawa Point station at ten o'clock that evening and all were on the road to recovery. The injured mate had his leg attended to by a local doctor and everyone got dry clothing supplied to the station from the Woman's National Relief Fund. Two weeks later, Mowat's body washed ashore near the wreck site and was buried by the local undertaker. The two schooner-barges simply went to pieces where they were.

Time passes and much is lost or forgotten. The shifting sand caused Au Sable Point to grow and shift by several hundred feet. The place where Daniel Mowat was buried has long been forgotten. Keeper Ocha headed into Tawas one night to visit his family. After the visit he set off on his boat to return to the station and simply vanished. All that was ever found of him was his hat, floating on Tawas Bay. Finally, both the *Midnight* and the *Mears* were forgotten. That is, until Cailen O'Shea discovered that caulking mallet 109 years later. As the 1990s turned into the 2000s the water levels in the Great Lakes went into one of their low cycles and the parts of the wrecks began to appear. Not knowing what they were, local folks had been gathering their parts for years, using them for bonfires. Then in 2000 the keel of the *Mears* surfaced. The site is now under careful archeological study by a team lead by Dr. O'Shea and all that can be found is being documented. The purpose of this story is to document what can not be seen today. That is the time of courage and valor when a community joined, hand in hand, with the Life Saving Service to rescue 11 souls from Lake Huron and a Thanksgiving dinner that officially lived up to its name.

The Haunting Of Hugh McKenna

Almost silently, the big steel car ferry *Badger* moves from her slip on a fine Ludington morning. Aboard are dozens of passengers and in her hold, where railroad cars once were carried, a parking lot of automobiles and trucks of all sorts now reside. Past the Coast Guard station and lighthouse the *Badger* steams as all aboard her experience the thrill of a crossing voyage. From early spring until late fall the *Badger* silently plows her way across Lake Michigan carrying more than 600 passengers at a time. Down on her car deck she also carries all of the cars, trucks and motor homes that those passengers have brought with them. In times past, that deck space was lined with rails to allow railroad freight cars to make the passage aboard this vessel. In the mid 1970s, however, the business of the railroads could no longer support cross-lake traffic and the days of the *Badger* appeared to be numbered. It was then that the concept of hauling passengers and automobiles across the lake gained favor. Many thought that the *Badger* and her managers could not make the cross-lake business profitable, that was in 1991. A decade later the *Badger* often sails with a sold-out crowd. It is the absolute best way to get from one side of Lake Michigan to the other.

Passage aboard the *Badger* cuts as much as six hours off of a trip around the lake as well as doing away with the insanity of navigating the highways around metropolitan Chicago. The entire trip on the *Badger* takes four hours and within the first hour the shoreline of Michigan is rapidly fading away into the horizon. A relaxed calmness settles in aboard the boat. Although there is a gift shop, maritime museum and two snack bars aboard the *Badger*, most of the passengers crowd the open deck and nearly every available deck chair soon contains a slumbering passenger. Other passengers peer over the rail and down toward the blue lake. As if trying to see as far into the mysterious depths as their imaginations can take them, some seem fixated. Perhaps they are simply stunned by the purity of the lake or maybe they are looking beyond the water toward people and events of the past. The passengers of the *Badger* would do well to look closely as the car ferry nears mid lake, because in these depths there are many stories and some of them are ghost stories.

Sometimes a ghost story can more clearly describe the sorrow of living rather than the sadness of death. Such was the case of poor Hugh McKenna. Not much is known about Hugh because in 1901, the era in which this story takes place, few records were kept as to the comings and goings of average folks. This was a time before Social Security numbers and before income taxes. It was a time when people were often born without having a birth certificate issued. It was also a time when immigrants from all around the world were flocking to America. Places such as Buffalo, New York were saturated with all sorts of people with all sorts of backgrounds. In the social static that clouded everyday of life in Buffalo, many folks had come from "the old country" and had nothing to cling to other than their family. Sometimes that family unit consisted only of a very few people. In Hugh McKenna's world his only family and his entire world consisted of his sister.

Oddly, there are no records that lead to the existence of Hugh McKenna's sister. In fact, there is no record of the name of Hugh's sister. As the 1800s were turning into the 1900s, thousands of McKennas were transiting western New York State and making their way across the Great Lakes region and migrating on to settle in the western United States. Hugh and his sister were nothing more than two faces in the crowd. Still we are left with a newspaper account of Hugh's tragic and haunting story. It all begins in mid November of 1901.

It was the second week of the ill month of November and the big package steamer *Syracuse* was huddled under a grain elevator at Buffalo. The Dart legs were down in her hold still chewing away at her grain cargo as preparations were being made to stow her roll on package freight. November's bluster had been whipping the grain dust across the dock as the forlorn figure of a man came shuffling along the wharf. After talking to a few dock workers the dejected Irishman was pointed in the direction of the *Syracuse's* mate. In a subdued tone McKenna asked the mate for a job aboard the boat. The mate asked if McKenna had any sailing experience and the depressed immigrant answered that he did not. Then he went on to explain that he had come to Buffalo with his beloved sister and that she had recently taken ill. McKenna went on to tell of how he had spent every dollar that he could muster to save his sister, but it was not enough and the poor woman had recently died leaving him penniless and broken hearted. He was willing to do any sort of work. The *Syracuse's* mate took pity on the gloomy man and granted him a job aboard the boat. Of course vessels of the *Syracuse's* breed were always in need of extra hands and there was plenty of manual labor that required no seaman's skill. So it was that Hugh McKenna came into the employ of the Western Transit Company and became a member of the crew of the *Syracuse*. It was an insignificant event that nearly everyone aboard the boat would soon come to regret.

No one really marked the departure of the *Syracuse* from the harbor of Buffalo. She had been making regular runs between Buffalo and the western ports of Lake Michigan for the Western Transit Company since 1884 and passage was so common as to be nearly unnoticed. As her 267-foot long iron hull pushed out onto Lake Erie, November's chop seemed to do little more than wash away some of the grain dust. Her destination on this trip was Milwaukee, Wisconsin and aboard the boat everyone seemed to settle into their normal routine–everyone that is, except Hugh McKenna. Several members of the boat's regular crew took notice that McKenna seemed to have an odd tendency to wonder the decks and mumble to himself. Some found it slightly amusing while others found it just plain strange. Most tried just to ignore him. Transients were common in this era of lakes sailing and every now and then an "odd duck" would get signed aboard. Normally such people would be onboard for a trip or two and then fade into the harbor background as easily as they appeared.

It took the *Syracuse* a full day to cross Lake Erie and another full day to snake her way up the Detroit and St. Clair rivers and into Lake Huron. In these hours of sailing there are plenty of tasks for the hands to tend to. After 16 seasons of hauling cargoes across the lakes, a boat such as the *Syracuse* needed plenty of care and little tasks such as chipping and painting took up most of the spare time. Western Transit always liked their vessels to remain spotless and it was up to the vessels first mate to assign the chores that assured that the company would remain happy. By the time that the *Syracuse* had reached the upper lakes, the mate had received several complaints that McKenna was not sticking to his work. He tended to stop and simply gaze off in odd directions and often held loud conversations with no one at all. Often he would simply wonder off and when asked where he was going he would say that he was going off to search for his sister.

Before long, the mate decided to have a talk with McKenna and set the situation straight. When the mate approached McKenna the delusional Irishman excitedly claimed that he had just seen his sister. After a protracted period of scolding, the mate saw that there was no way to get through to McKenna and resigned to simply discharge him when the boat reached Milwaukee.

As time went on, McKenna grew more and more unbalanced. He would grab fellow crew members and indicate that his dead sister was standing "right over there." Of course they would see nothing when they looked where he was pointing. Soon these antics went from an annoying game to plain craziness. Crewmen would simply stand and shake their heads as McKenna saw his sister's ghost over and over again. Once in the middle of the night, McKenna suddenly climbed the boat's forward mast. Fortunately, the mate was on duty and not the captain. If the old man had seen this he would surely have blown his stack and it would have been the mate who took the guff because it was he that signed McKenna onto the crew. Of course, no one dared to go up and get McKenna because in his state of mind he may just fall and take someone with him. Shouting at him was out of the question because the raised voices may wake the captain. All that the mate could do was hope that this nut came down before morning. Eventually, McKenna climbed down complaining that he had followed his sister up the spar, but she had gotten away before he could catch her. The mate decided that enough was enough and had two crewmen hustle him down into the fo'c'sle and lock him up.

For a while, things got back to normal aboard the *Syracuse*. The boat threaded her way through the Straits of Mackinaw and began to cross the expanse of upper Lake Michigan. A powerful gale was blowing across all of the upper lakes and northern Lake Michigan was getting a good taste of it. The sturdy hull of the *Syracuse* was making good weather in the seas as she steamed in mid lake somewhere between Manitowoc and Ludington. Rolling waves and spitting snow lashed at the steamer, but had no ill effect. The boat's mate was working below decks with his able bodied seamen at the chore of keeping the cargo stable. No one bothered to ask if McKenna was going to pitch in. No one dared. He was safely tucked away and hopefully the storm would keep him there. With any luck the Irishman who had never sailed before would be struck with a bad case of seasickness and have his head stuck in a bucket until the boat reached Milwaukee.

Such was not to be the case, as Hugh McKenna's sister appeared to him once again. This time she found him in his bunk. With a pretty smile she beckoned to him as her ghostly image slipped toward the cabin door and then melted through it. McKenna was crazed, he got the door opened and leaped into the companionway. There at the end of the hall she moved as if leading him. Out onto the deck she flew playfully and McKenna chased after her as if they were again children in Ireland. Down the length of the pitching deck they both went and up the companionway that led to the aft cabin's roof. In a ghostly game of tag she began to lead him around the smokestacks. Around and around they went as he shouted to her and reached out to touch her once again. Up in the pilothouse, the captain had taken notice, for the first time, of this odd crewman's behavior.

"Who's that?" he asked the wheelsman.

"Some odd fellow that signed aboard in Buffalo." The wheelsman replied.

"Tell the mate to get back there and catch that madman." The captain directed as he took the wheel himself.

McKenna, however, would not give anyone the chance to catch him. He was going to catch the ghost of his sister and he was going to do it right now. With a leap he dashed from the *Syracuse's* deckhouse roof and directly into Lake Michigan.

In shock the captain ordered the engine checked down and began to turn the boat as he blew a distress signal on the boat's steam whistle. Below decks the mate felt the boat shudder and turn. Then he heard the throaty howl of the whistle belching the danger signal. In an instant he knew that this was not a shipwreck–it was Hugh McKenna. Out onto the open deck the entire crew mustered as the captain shouted from up on the bridge wing "man overboard!"

"Should be madman overboard." The mate muttered out of the side of his mouth.

No amount of searching could find Hugh McKenna and in weather this rough there was little point in trying. Soon the *Syracuse* was put back on her course and in a few hours she passed safely into Milwaukee.

In the pilothouse the mate had plenty of explaining to do. He told the captain as little as possible and briefly stated that he had taken pity on the poor soul in Buffalo and the man had simply gone mad with grief over his sister's death. Without doubt there were some words about being more careful as to what kind of people are enlisted as crew and the matter was then dropped. Another crewman would be signed aboard in Milwaukee and it is a sure bet that his sanity was closely examined.

There is no way to be sure that Hugh McKenna was the name of the man who chased the ghost off of the *Syracuse* on that stormy day in November of 1901. In that era, vagabonds often signed aboard vessels using assumed names. There is also no way to know for absolute certainty that the man in question actually had a sister that died or if she was simply an ongoing delusion of his. We know for sure only that a man who called himself Hugh McKenna chased a ghost that he believed was his sister overboard and into eternity from the roof of the *Syracuse*. Still, if you are taking the *Badger* across Lake Michigan, you may be able to peer down into the depths and see a happy Irishman and his adored sister reunited forever. Look closely those of you who would cross the lake aboard this silent ferryboat, because indeed there are many stories out on the open lake, and some of those are ghost stories.

Let Her Perish

Sometimes the same circumstances that lead a person to the bottle can also lead them to seek a job at sea. In fact the abuse of alcohol has been around as long as civilization. The causes are debated as being anything from a weak soul to a genetic predisposition. In modern times we discuss alcohol abuse as a disease and often provide assorted social programs to aid its victims while using the most politically correct terms to describe them. Oddly it is only in the stringent rehabilitation programs such as Alcoholics Anonymous that members are commonly found to refer to their peers as "drunks." Such was actually the common term used in the less enlightened days of the past. Had you been a visitor aboard the Canadian schooner *Sweet Home* while she sat at the wharf Mill Point, Ontario in the autumn of 1878, you may well have heard the boat's first mate, John Nix refer to the boat's cook, Norah Spellman in those terms. In fact, the entire crew often grumbled in subdued voices and described her as "Nothin' but a blasted drunk." This time and place were a long way from today's modern compassion.

Just what drove Norah Spellman to seek her salvation at the bottom of a bottle is not on record. Likewise, what caused her to seek employment as a cook on a lakeboat is not on record. There is the possibility that these two aspects of her life have the same cause or that the motivation for one event caused the other. What is on record is that Captain Richard Charles, master of the schooner *Sweet Home*, had signed Norah aboard as cook at her request and she occupied that position in the autumn of 1878.

Having a female cook on a lake vessel was a trend that dated back as far as the earliest days of navigation on the fresh water seas. In fact, there was a boom in the popularity of such employment that seems to have taken place in the years following the civil war. Female cooks, it was found, worked for less money and tended to create better food than their male counterparts. For many ladies of the lakes, the job as a cook on a lakeboat represented adventure and travel and often better pay than jobs ashore. Keep in mind that the late 1800s were a time when travel was not as common as it is today. A trip of just fifty miles was an adventure and many folks lived their entire life without ever traveling beyond such a distance. Going aboard a lakeboat meant the opportunity to see the big cities such as Detroit, Chicago, Toronto, Cleveland and Buffalo. In the space of a few years a young lady could see more places than her peers back home would likely see in a lifetime. A job aboard a lake vessel was also an adventure. There was danger in working the lakes as each season there were hundreds and sometimes thousands of people who perished in those icy waters. A lady who survived could spend the rest of her life telling thrilling tales of her true adventures on the Great Lakes. To many of the young ladies the job as ship's cook also meant escape. Escape from the pressures of life ashore and escape from the many hens who would peck at the lifestyle of a young maiden of this era. If a woman were to pass into her late 20s and not be married and productively raising a family, the hens would begin to peck at her. Terms like "Old Maid" were often applied in whispers that could easily be heard from a distance. Questions such as "What's wrong?" were asked in ways that only the hens could manage. The thoughts that perhaps a young lady simply wanted to live her own life or simply have her independence were lost in the pressure to maintain the social status quo. There was also the escape of the terrors of an abusive home life. Abuses that we will not detail here were escaped by shipping out on a lakeboat.

Of course there were those who spoke out from the female "mainstream" about this potentially sordid type of employment. Remember, this was an era when the thought of a unwed man and a woman on a carriage ride without an escort was considered to be near scandalous. The thought of a lone female confined aboard a vessel far from civilization with all of those men was simply too shocking. Why the temptations must surely be overwhelming. Letters to the editors of port city newspapers often complained about this immoral practice and the types of women that would seek such employment. Still, in spite of the myopic hens, there were plenty of ladies who shipped out aboard lakeboats and found honorable work and the respect of their fellow crew members as well as their sister cooks. In fact, from the records and old newspapers, it appears as if a silent sisterhood was formed among the female cooks. On several occasions, these ladies of the lakes actually went on strike to demand a pay rate similar to that of male cooks. Even though nearly every vessel on which these female cooks were employed was an independently owned and operated business, the lady cooks got what they were demanding. In retrospect, we can say that the reasons why these lady cooks had shipped aboard their respective lakeboats were as varied as the personalities of the ladies themselves.

What brought Norah aboard the *Sweet Home* was known only to her and her use of the bottle to the point of being labeled "a drunk" was her own business as well. We can speculate, but we would likely be wrong. The reasons could vary from an abusive upbringing to a propensity toward seasickness. To John Nix and the rest of the crew of the *Sweet Home*, Norah's reasons did not matter. She had been crawling into the bottle all season and they had paid the price with their stomachs. Drunks tend to cook very poor meals and a lakeboat runs on the stomachs of its crew. Although no one kept a log of it, we can guess that her meals had tended toward being more slop than food. Captain Charles was reluctant to fire his sloshed cook because it would be hard to find a replacement so late in the season. Actually, it was probably fairly hard to find any female cook who would sign aboard the *Sweet Home*. The boat itself was old, small and it smelled bad. Measuring just 98 feet long and 21 feet in beam the crew's quarters that the boat provided were cramped to say the least. Worst of all, when the boat had been constructed at Oshawa, Ontario in 1853, no accommodation was ever considered for housing a female crew member. The cook's "quarters" at best would be a small, closet-sized area with a bunk and, probably, a simple curtain for privacy. The biggest discomfort had to be the lady's bathroom–because there was none. Onboard a sailing vessel of this era, the crewmen simply went to the forward rigging and "went" in the water. For a lady the best that could be had was a simple bucket whose contents were then tossed overboard. Bathing was simply not done. If you wanted to wash up, you would take another bucket and put it over the side, pulling back aboard clean water to wash with. It was obviously important for a lady to have different buckets and know which was which.

Another aspect that had probably kept Norah aboard *Sweet Home* in spite of her drinking was the vessel's cargo scheduling. Scrounging up cargos for the boat to haul required Captain Charles to travel from one port to another and personally huckster individual deals. This meant that he spent most of his time on trains or walking city streets and sleeping in hotels rather than aboard the boat. So his contact with Norah and her slop was quite limited. Most of what he knew came from John Nix as he complained on behalf of the crew.

On November 28th, Captain Charles was in Kingston, Ontario meeting with the owner of the *Sweet Home*, Benjamin Barney, who had managed to swing a deal with E.W. Rathbun & Company. The deal was for the *Sweet Home* to haul 10,600 board-feet of Canadian lumber down from Mill Point to Oswego, New York. Captain Charles sent a telegram from Kingston and instructed First Mate Nix to make the trip without delay. With that in hand, Nix got the boat underway and headed south across Lake Ontario.

A nasty dawn was breaking across the western end of Lake Ontario on November 29, 1878. The weather that day was typical for the end of November and at Oswego's east pier watchman Thomas Keeliher was just about to finish his night's work. Although the wind had churned up a rude sea that was rolling nearly due east, the dark gray clouds were not yet spitting out any snow. Heeled over on her port side, the *Sweet Home* was beating her way toward the inner harbor and making the best use of the wind all the way in. Having just the mainsail and two jibs up, the little two masted schooner appeared about to make the port with ease. Standing by, the tug *Morey* was ready to take a line and escort the *Sweet Home* into the dock.

Although all appeared to be going smoothly from the outside, on the inside of the *Sweet Home's* cabin it was a different matter. Norah had gotten into her bottle on the trip across and was making a drunken annoyance of herself. It was sure that there would be no breakfast aboard the *Sweet Home* this morning. Some of the boat's crew probably talked about leaving the boat when they tied up rather than work at the unloading on an empty belly again. Nix himself was at his limit with Norah's drunkenness and honestly wished to be rid of her.

Then, just as the tug took up the line of the *Sweet Home*, Lake Ontario stepped in to solve the problem once and for all. With a huff of its November breath the icy lake reached out and snapped the line between the tug and the schooner. A line that the schooner had been using all season and appeared to be trustworthy suddenly went slack and dropped to the bottom of the harbor. This all happened just as her crew was occupied with the freshly lowered sails and suddenly the *Sweet Home* was at the mercy of the merciless lake. In a scramble the sailors hustled to retrieve their line while the tug came in close and tossed them one of her lines. Making the tug's line secure, the crew of the *Sweet Home* were allowed just a moment of ease before the lake reached out and snapped that line too. Before another line could be exchanged the waves and wind carried the old schooner stern-first into the piles of the east pier. With a sickening crunch the aft timbers of the boat were crushed in and a deluge of ice water cascaded into Norah's drunken world. With surprising speed the *Sweet Home* spun around as she was blown along the pier until her telephone pole sized jib boom caught in the piles. With a resounding "crack" the boom snapped as the bowsprit was carried away.

Thinking fast Nix and the three other men who made up the boat's sober crew, leaped to the dock when the *Sweet Home* struck it and left both the schooner and its drunken cook in the custody of Lake Ontario. Watchman Keeliher saw the entire wreck and came running up to the four sailors. He asked if everyone had gotten off of the boat. They answered that everyone had gotten off except the cook. Keeliher was stunned and in an instant began to run down the wharf shouting that he was going to get the lifesavers to come out and save the cook. To his disbelief he heard Nix shout back, "She's a drunk. Let her perish!"

At the Oswego Life Saving Station, Keeper Blackburn had been awakened by the sound of the *Sweet Home's* jib boom snapping and already had his crew mustered as Keeliher reached the station door. Unaware that the crew was mustered in the boat room, at first Keeliher knocked, and later began kicking the station door trying to gain their attention. Finally one of the crew came out and told him that they were about to launch their boat and to stand back. By this time the *Sweet Home* had been blown into the shallows a few hundred feet east of the station and was rapidly breaking up. The lifesavers did not have far to row before reaching the boat. Once there they found Norah sloshing around in a drunken confusion and they easily removed her from the wreck. From the pier the crew of the schooner watched as the lifesavers poured Norah into their surfboat and then rowed away.

"Looks like they got her." One of the crew grumbled.

"Yep," Nix muttered, "too bad."

That was the end of the schooner *Sweet Home*. She broke up in place and her bones are buried in the lake bottom to this day. We do not know whatever became of Norah Spellman, but we can guess that she went back into her bottle and eventually found her end there. The use of female cooks on Great Lakes freighters continued in spite of the hens and their highbrowed objections. In fact, the role of females on the lakes continued into modern times. Lakeboats still employ female crew members today. The difference now is that they are not confined to the job of "cook." Today the modern ladies of the lakes do every job from captain to engineer to cook. Their reasons for shipping out on a lakeboat are more professional than personal today and for the most part they work with their male counterparts as equals. In another evolution of the lakes shipping industry, the use of alcohol by crew members onboard lakeboats is strictly forbidden and that rule is heavily enforced. Whether it had been seasickness or personal problems that lead Norah Spellman to drink, her activity would not have allowed her to serve aboard a modern lakeboat with the professionals who are today's ladies of the lakes.

Bones In The Backwaters

Just off of Morton Street, on the southwest end of Bay City, Michigan an obscure softball park comes to life each spring as amateur players clad in their lucky shirts and soiled cleats greet the first days of fair weather. Through the summer the park comes to life almost daily as the season is played out. Bats smack the softball as players scramble, whistle and shout. Occasionally a well slammed ball soars over the right field fence and bounces toward the riverbank which is poised just behind the ball field. A loyal spectator or player will trot to the resting place of the worn white ball, recover the pill and toss it back over the fence, giving quiet thanks that the ball did not roll down the steep riverbank and into the swampy mudflat beyond. Curiously, each time that this happens, the person who shags the wayward ball misses the opportunity to discover a long forgotten shipwreck which has rested near that same riverbank for more than 125 years. We cannot blame the people of summer for missing this ghost from our maritime past, because the wreck has a tendency to hide on bright summer days and seems to only reveal itself when the skies turn gloomy gray and the winds blow a gale from the south. It is only then that the murky waters of the river will drop and expose the dark muddy bottom and the brooding skeleton of a once proud vessel whose useful days are now forgotten. There, in the smelly muck she lies quietly wishing for her story to be told.

Darkness had already set in across the lumber mills of Bay City by the time that the side wheel tug *Katy Reid* dropped her raft of logs at the Wooden Ware Works. It was just after nine o'clock on the autumn evening of Wednesday, October 29, 1873 and this was the golden era of the lumber industry on the Saginaw River. Once the float of logs was secured, Captain Henry Vosburg shouted down toward Engineer Lemuel Maxfield to "back her", and the engineer ratcheted the *Katy Reid's* steam engine to meet the captain's orders. Small tugs such as the *Reid* were the workhorses of the river and their propulsion equipment was often simple. Normally, a side wheel tug of the *Katy Reid's* class would be equipped with a steam engine of the sort common to railroad locomotives of the same era. Easy to obtain and maintain, these engines consisted of a single cylinder mounted horizontally on the upper deck or on a mid-deck. Although there are no records which specifically say the exact type of power plant that was actually built into the *Reid*, the records that have been discovered state that she had a single steam cylinder that measured 16 inches in diameter with a 55 inch stroke, which would be consistent with a railroad type steam plant. Although we do not know a lot about the *Katy Reid's* engine, you can bet that on that October night in 1873, Engineer Lem Maxfield knew every hiss and thump of that vessel's engine by heart.

Records conflict as to the *Katy Reid's* exact location of construction by saying that she was built at DePere or Green Bay. Her year of construction has been listed as 1867 and she was originally entered into the short-haul passenger trade. This trade lead her to work upon Michigan's Grand River. She served in that capacity only a short time, however, and was pressed into service as a towing tug in 1871. With the opening of the 1872 sailing season the little boat was sold to John D. McKinnon for $7,000 and brought to the Saginaw River to work out of Bay City. McKinnon had her twin boilers replaced that same season with a single boiler. It is likely that he did this not because the boat's boilers were wearing out, but because the original boilers were unsafe. The boilers that were

Sidewheel tug Katy Reid *shown here on the Saginaw River.*
Author's composite.

placed in small "back yard built" steamers of this era were like ticking time bombs. Often they tended to explode for apparently no reason at all. Replacing them with quality marine boilers, of which there were many available in Bay City area, would be a move toward increasing the life expectancy and value of the boat. In fact, after having changed the boilers, McKinnon then increased the *Reid's* value from $7,000 to $12,000. It would appear that Mr. McKinnon had a long and profitable career mapped out for the little tug, but what he really had in mind was to attract a buyer for the vessel. So it was that she was sold to a budding Bay City lumber baron named George Campbell. Along with the little boat came her captain and chief engineer, both of whom were added to the Campbell payroll. Unfortunately, Mr. Campbell's time with the *Katy Reid* would be very limited.

As soon as the *Reid* had her heels in the open channel, Captain Vosburg shouted down to bring her ahead and once more Lem ratcheted her engine to meet the command. With a rhythmic series of splashes the buckets of the tug's 16 foot diameter paddle wheels dug into the river's surface and churned the *Katy Reid* ahead. Each paddle blade, which were properly called "buckets", measured five feet, four inches wide and 17 inches tall so they managed to get a good bite on the water. As he wheeled the tug's barn-door style rudder and directed her bow, Captain Vosburg pointed the *Katy Reid* toward the west draw of the Lafayette Street bridge and a section of the river known as the "West Channel." This area of the Saginaw River is bisected by an elongated sliver of an island known as the "Middle Grounds" and in the *Katy Reid's* day the entire area was a clutter of saw mills, salt works, hoop mills and the assorted docks that would support the river's industry. It was Captain Vosburg's intention to moor his tug at Staudacher's Dock for the night and that pier was nestled in the confines of the West Channel.

Although the waters of the West Channel were shallow, Captain Vosburg routinely took the *Katy Reid* in and out of there without an afterthought. Side wheel tugs such as the *Reid* were specifically designed and constructed with operations in shallow water in mind. The *Katy Reid* herself measured out at 101 feet in length and 17 feet in beam, not counting her paddle-boxes. Her depth, however, was a minimal six feet six inches meaning that she probably drew something in the neighborhood of two feet of water. Closing in on the swing bridge, the *Reid's* captain gave a toot on the boat's steam whistle signaling the bridge tender to open and let the boat pass. It was a routine that the bridge tenders of this era went through as many as 100 times each day. From tugs to schooners to the big lumber hookers, there was plenty of water traffic to swing the bridge for. Vehicular traffic was another matter. It would be another 40 years before the automobile would become accessible to the average person and even buggy traffic was limited to the "well to do" people of Bay City and Salzburg. Thus the only "traffic" that the swinging of the bridge would disrupt would be that of people crossing the river on foot. In short order the bridge was swinging open and the *Reid* was slipping through with the only noise being that of her paddle wheels.

As Captain Vosburg guided the *Reid* up to Staudacher's dock and had her lines made secure, he saw that a large pile of cordwood was stacked upon the dock. In this era, vessels such as the *Katy Reid* were fueled with wood rather than coal. Wood was far more plentiful and far cheaper to use and the *Reid's* boiler was well heated with it. Along the Saginaw River, like many other waterways on the lakes, local farmers knew that a handy way to supplement their income was to cut the trees on their land and then sell the wood to steamer captains as fuel. One such local farmer was Bartholomew Staudacher, a man who was rapidly moving from the role of sod buster to the role of entrepreneur in 1873. He not only owned the dock where the *Katy Reid* had tied up, but also owned a local farm, a local salt works and a dry goods store located less than a mile from the dock. In the future, Mr. Staudacher would acquire property to the point where he would own most of the land and buildings from the foot of the Lafayette Street bridge along Salzburg Road to the city line. For the moment, however, Mr. Staudacher's concern was in selling Captain Vosburg the wood needed to fuel the *Katy Reid*. For the better part of the next two hours, countless split logs were passed from one callused hand to another as it went aboard the *Reid*. Finally, with the fuel stacked upon her deck, the *Katy Reid* was considered to be fully "wooded up" and ready for the next day's toil. It was just before midnight when her crew turned in for a well deserved night's sleep. Once all items aboard the tug were checked as secure, and the last oil lamp had been extinguished, the *Katy Reid* herself seemed to breathe a long sigh of relieved slumber.

On the other side of the West Channel from Staudacher's Dock, clad in his heavy uniform coat and English "Bobby-style" policeman's cap, a local patrolman walked his beat watchful of all that was around him. The Bay City waterfront was rough place in the mid-1800s and the officer's night-stick had its share of scars and could likely tell more than a few stories of rowdy sailors and wayward ladies of the night who were delivered a dose of on the spot justice. Tonight, however, the streets were quiet and the waterfront was unusually peaceful. Then, just before three o'clock the patrolman's instinct began to tell him that something was amiss. He listened, he sniffed the autumn air and he began to look around himself. Across the river he saw the cause of his apprehension. Over there, by the dock, a vessel was on fire! He knew that men were aboard asleep and as he looked toward the flames of the *Katy Reid*, he saw that the fire was practically exploding in its growth. In the context of 1873, the number 911 would be best defined as the number of heart beats that it would take for anyone to sound any type of alarm or summon any sort of help rather than the number that you use to call for help. There were no cell phones, no emergency operators and no radio dispatched fire departments, there were only the people that you could shout to who could be of any sort of help in an emergency. In order to reach the burning vessel, the officer would have to run almost a mile to the bridge, then cross the river and run another near mile to Staudacher's dock. The only other person awake in the area would be the bridge tender, that is, provided he was not asleep at the switch. As the shocked policeman sprinted toward the bridge he clenched his whistle in his teeth and blew its alarm into the once quiet night as if to wake the dead, or at least wake someone closer to the *Katy Reid* than the opposite shore of the river. Running toward the bridge he kept looking back across the river only to see the flames growing at a fearful rate. In the deep darkness of that autumn night, that lone policeman found himself awake in a nightmare, the tug *Katy Reid* and her crew were being incinerated and he was apparently the only person on earth who knew it was happening, yet he could do nothing to help. By the time that the exhausted officer dashed the distance to the bridge, the bridge tender was out of his cab and the two of them stood looking toward the wooden tug which was now afire from end to end …it appeared to be too late.

What the patrolman and the bridge tender could not know was that shortly after the fire had broken out, someone aboard the *Katy Reid* had been awakened by the smoke and managed to alert the rest of the crew. They were aroused not a moment too soon as the fire had started somewhere in the upper works and threatened to trap them all below. All aboard the tug escaped with only the clothing on their backs with the exception of one man. That lone crewman did manage to escape, but without any clothing at all on his back. Clad only in his birthday suit the crewman dove into the shallow muddy river to escape the flames.

The patrolman who had first spotted the fire attempted to summon the steam fire engine from the Seventh Ward firehouse, but they said that the burning vessel was not in their jurisdiction and refused to turn out. The fact is that in 1873 there was no fire fighting equipment of any sort anywhere near the location where the *Katy Reid* was burning. It is likely that an effort was made to cut her free from the dock and thus save the pier, but other than that, all that could be done was to allow the *Reid* to burn down to the waterline where the river would then flow in and snuff the fire. By dawn, all that remained of the tug was her metal boiler, engine and side wheel frames as well as about a foot and a half of her hull which was now submerged into the muddy bottom. George Campbell had insured the boat, but only for the sum of $7,000 and had taken a loss in the fire of $5,000. No one ever determined what had started the fire that consumed the *Katy Reid* to the waterline, but everyone was thankful that no one had died. Her captain and engineer were left to find other work and one of her crew was left to find other clothing. There after life went on and in a very short time the dealings of Great Lakes maritime history quickly overshadowed the little lost tugboat. Eventually the *Katy Reid* was totally forgotten.

Events involving the remains of the *Katy Reid* after the fire are nearly undocumented with only one repeated paragraph in the maritime sections of local papers to be found. It states that her boiler was removed and placed in the tug *A.H. Hunter* in March of 1874. One other secondhand reference states that her remains were removed and turned into a lighter. This is thought to be in error or simply false because when a side wheel tug is burned to the water line, extremely little of the hull is likely to remain. As the decades passed the sands of time as well as the silt of the Saginaw River soon swallowed the bones of the *Katy Reid* and the little tug was completely forgotten. Over the decades, several wars were fought, the nation's economy collapsed and recovered a few times and the salt industry, lumber industry and tugboat industry all vanished from the Saginaw River. The west draw of the Lafayette Street bridge was replaced by a permanently closed span, effectively cutting off the West Channel to navigation. This really made no difference, because by the 1920s vessels no longer went in there anyhow. During the era of the "Great Depression" of the 1930s, the last remains of the saw mills in the area were swept away from the Middle Grounds and West

Stern of the wrecked tug Katy Reid. *D.J. Story photo.*

Wreckage of the Katy Reid *as seen at low water. D.J. Story photo.*

Channel. From that point on the West Channel became nothing more than simply a murky, overgrown and forgotten backwater of the Saginaw River.

For as long as most boat nuts who are local to the Bay City area can remember, there have been rumors of "old wooden shipwrecks" in that backwater of the Middle Grounds. Normally these rumors would always start with " ...a guy who used to work on a dredge back in the 30s or 40s said..." and had the result of being shrugged off as nothing more than tall tales. Finally, a Bay City maritime historian, Don Comtois, decided to take it upon himself to find out if all of this was true and one winter day when the winds were blowing strong from the southwest and the river was exceptionally low he went to the West Channel and found the long rumored wreck. In November of 2001 the author of this book and his research buddy D.J. Story decided to use the historically low levels of the Great Lakes waters as well as that of the Saginaw River and explore Don's wreck. Because of that effort, you too can now rediscover the wreck of the *Katy Reid.*

Walking past the vacant softball park, which was closed for the winter, you come to the bank of the river. A drop of over six feet leads down to the mudflat. The riverbank itself is lined

Wreckage of Katy Reid *arcs into the mud. This view is looking forward toward the bow.* Author's photo.

with rip-rap stone and the discarded bricks of burned buildings that once stood on the shore. There, laying somewhat flattened in the mud rest the bones of what was the *Katy Reid*. At first it appears to be some sort of old wooden piles or an abandoned dock, but upon closer examination the outline of a vessel becomes apparent. The arc of the hull leading to the bow and the rows of ribs become obvious once the care is taken to notice them. Although there is no modern record to pinpoint it, months of research revealed that the location of this wreckage is in the spot where Staudacher's dock was likely to have been located. The vessel's timbers clearly show that these remains were burned as each rib appears as if it has been sliced off nearly even with every other rib, a trait that indicates rapid sinking while being burned. The ribs are all made up of double "futtocks," which is the name for the individual timbers that are used to construct a vessel's ribs. Each futtock is a three inch timber fastened to its mate by a longitudinal wrought iron bolt. One individual rib is missing half of its width, but the longitudinal bolt that held the two futtocks together juts out and

Image showing the stem-iron of the Katy Reid's *wreckage.*
D.J. Story photo.

remains unbent which is another telltale sign of a burned vessel. The ribs themselves are spaced on 24 inch centers and are of lightweight construction having fewer bolts than larger vessels such as schooners or lumber hookers. The remains of the hull arc toward a bow which has a rounded forefoot and an iron plate known as a "stem-iron" attached to it. Both of these traits are consistent with the vessel being a tug.

Laying in the water just aft of amidships of the wreck and positioned at almost 90 degrees to the main hull is the stern section. This piece gives the appearance of having been torn away from the rest of the hull as if to gain access to the wreck's boiler and engine. This too is consistent with the story of the *Katy Reid* as it would be an indication of a quick and dirty salvage of a boiler and engine from a burned steamer. One inconsistency is a strange "bow" of metal bands that support some sort of canister-shaped object at the after most end of the stern. If this is a stern tube, it would indicate that this piece is that of a propeller, and the records clearly show that the *Reid* was a side wheeler. If, however, this object is a rudder bearing that has been bent upward in the act of pulling the hull apart, it could belong to a side wheeler. Both the length and beam of the wreckage are consistent with the *Katy Reid*, but much of the hull is either buried or under water and accurate measurements have yet to be taken. So low is the wreck, that if the river is at its normal level the timbers are completely hidden, so chances to study and document large portions of the vessel are rare. So murky is the water in this area that when it again covers the wreck you can stand with your toes within one inch of where you know a piece of the *Reid* is located and you can see no sign of her at all.

For everyone who has done any study of Great Lakes shipping history, the dream of stumbling upon an old, forgotten wooden shipwreck is a reoccurring event. So, to push through the brush and stumble down the river bank and visit the *Katy Reid* is a special event. Often the water covers her and there is no sign of her grave at all, but sometimes she shows herself and lets us ponder her existence and her short career. She may have been an insignificant boat in her time, but she is indeed a maritime historian's dream come true today. The mud that surrounds the hull is so polluted and filled with disease causing organisms that the boat's remains will never be excavated. In that mud, however, are all of the artifacts that were not consumed in the fire. Like a toxic time capsule from 1873, the site of the wreck holds everything that the crew would have used from eye glasses to dishes. Of course, what researcher would be crazy enough to dig into the muck of the Middle Grounds to look for such things?

Oddly, unlike other wrecks of the Great Lakes, the *Katy Reid* is not protected by the Bottomlands Preservation act. Wrecks located in Michigan's rivers are not protected by such law. Of course the *Katy Reid* is, as of this writing, in no real danger of being disturbed. Her grave is in an isolated backwater that is used only by an occasional carp fisherman and the adjacent property is something less than prime real estate. The

Satellite photo showing the location of the Katy Reid's *wreckage. U.S. Geological Survey.*

odds are that the *Katy Reid* will rest where she is for a very long time to come.

In recorded maritime history, there have been hundreds of vessels that were either wrecked or abandoned on the Saginaw River, yet a careful accounting of the records shows only one that is positively identified as being in the West Channel of the Middle Grounds and that is the *Katy Reid.* Although without finding a name board or some other artifact that absolutely identifies the bones in this backwater, there will always be some who may question her exact identity. Any of these skeptics who may scoff at this story are more than welcome to go to the boat's grave and dig for conclusive evidence. There is, however, one fact that will continue to be true, and that is that every summer the softball players will run, hit and shout within a few yards of an old wooden shipwreck, yet be unaware that she lays there, within walking distance of their playing field.

Escape From Murray's Nightmare

For Frank Murray, first mate of the schooner *Plover*, standing watch at the vessel's rail and looking down into the lake as the blue water rolled past was a favored place indeed. Tonight the vessel was gliding along under easy sail and he stood casually on her port quarter gazing down at the gentle waves. Suddenly, the water began to grow muddy and Murray thought that the boat may have strayed into shoal water or onto some unmarked shallow area. He tried to turn to shout to the wheelsman to turn the boat, but he could not move, he was paralyzed and unable to turn his gaze from the water below. Then he saw it, a face, ashen white it began to come toward the surface. As the face surfaced the eyes were wide open, glassy with both terror and death they seemed to look directly at him. It was then that Murray realized that the floating corpse had on his clothing. The face of the drown body was in fact his own face. Murray tried to run but was held to the rail as if frozen. In moments the waves tossed at the body playfully and then shoved it astern and out of sight, forever a possession of the cold dark lake. With a gasp, Murray lurched until he was sitting upright in his bunk covered in sweat with his heart pounding as if it would leap from his chest. All around the sounds of the *Plover* pleasantly sailing were heard and the midday sun streamed in through the cracks in the shutters. It was April 9, 1871, a fine spring Sunday and Murray had been having a simple bad dream as he dozed in an off duty nap. For the startled first mate, however, the entire event had been far too real to dismiss as a simple dream.

It is unlikely that by using any means of searching you will find persons more superstitious than mariners. For as long as there has been transportation by water there have been superstitions held by sailors. The Great Lakes are no exception to the influence of superstition. For example it is considered to be bad luck to depart a port on a Friday and lake captains in the era of wooden vessels were known to deliberately delay their departure until a few minutes past midnight, and thus sail on Saturday morning, to allow the hoodoo to pass. Rats seen leaving a vessel are considered to be a sign that the vessels will be lost on the next trip and crews, noticing rats departing, have been known to follow their example. Using the recovered equipment from a wreck is also thought to be an act that will bring bad luck. And also on the long list of bad luck makers were dreams. As Frank Murray came back on deck after his nap, he was still a bit disoriented from the experience. For a moment he probably expected to see his own body floating off behind in the wake of the *Plover*. As Murray came face to face with Captain Jones, he described his dream in the most quiet of tone, but in very urgent terms. The captain could see by the look on the mate's face that no spoken words were likely to convince him that it was just a dream. In fact, Murray gave all the appearance of a man that was frightened beyond the point of simple terror and nearly into a state of shock.

Through the rest of that day Captain Jones kept a close, but candid watch on his first mate. Murray paced the deck as if he expected the lake to simply reach out and snatch him at any moment. The shipping season had only been open for a few days at this time and with the previous winter having been a fair one, the lake waters were largely free of spring time ice so the *Plover* had gotten an early start to boot. If the first mate was going to be haunted in this manner, Captain Jones reckoned that it would be a long season to come. He hoped that Murray would snap out of it in a few days.

During dinner that night, Murray did little more than pick at his food. His strange behavior was beginning to attract the attention of the rest of the crew. Captain Jones decided to have another consultation with his distressed first mate. Murray still insisted that some sort of doom was hanging over him or worse yet hanging over the entire vessel and crew because of him. Captain Jones told him that such omens were just as probable to bring good luck as they were bad luck. His logic failed to reach Murray who now began to turn his panic attack back home and wondered aloud if something bad had not happened to his family. In modern times, such fears are easily removed with a simple telephone call or an e-mail, but in 1871 such methods of instant communication were unknown. In fact it would be another four years before Alexander Graham Bell would assemble the components that would allow a voice to be transmitted by wire and thus later create the telephone. So, when a mariner on an old wooden schooner out on the Great Lakes had a sense of dread about events back home, it could be weeks before word could be passed by letter or worse yet, the answer may have to wait until the close of the shipping season. Still, history shows us that in the season of 1871 there would be more than 1,160 vessel incidents on the lakes. More than 270 mariners would be lost in the season that was ahead of the *Plover*, so from our point of view Murray's paranoia may have just been good thinking.

Murray spent the rest of the day pacing the deck and then degraded into a resigned gloom of simply gazing overboard toward the lake. He knew that the April water was so cold that it was only slightly beyond being solid ice. A person finding themselves immersed in that water would live only a matter of minutes before the bitter cold would sap their life away. He knew also that the *Plover* herself was far from being a new boat. Having been launched in 1857 at Milan, Ohio the 390 ton schooner was getting up in years and also in mileage. Should a sudden spring gale come up, Murray could easily find himself becoming that corpse from his nightmare. Fortunately, by nightfall Captain Jones noticed that his first mate had settled down and was somewhat less distracted by the previous morning's bad dream. Yet, Murray refused to go to sleep before his late night watch. Captain Jones understood that there were just some things that will keep a sailor up at night.

At midnight, Captain Jones turned the watch over to Murray who was still tending to pace the deck a bit, but appeared to have his wits about him. All of the schooners lamps were properly set and the lookout was posted at the *Plover's* bow as the night began to pass quietly. Leaving the boat's wheel on the lash, Murray continued his troubled pacing of the deck. His mind raced around the images that had been in his dream and he wondered in a million different ways what they could mean. Shortly after two o'clock in the morning, as the *Plover* skimmed across upper Lake Huron the breeze began to freshen and with it the jib sail began to spill. Now Murray's concern turned from his nightmare to his night's duties. Leaving the wheel lashed, he headed forward to fix the jib. On his way Murray found the crewman on lookout and had him come along to assist in the rigging. Both men made their way out onto the bowsprit which involved placing their feet upon the lines that ran from the bow, out ahead on the *Plover* to align her jib boom which is the mast-like boom that extends forward of the vessel. This is the same area where the crew members go to "relieve" themselves and so even the greenest of sailors would be more than familiar with the traverse in all sorts of weather, day or night. As both men worked at the re-rig of the jib, the lookout was nearer the boat and Murray was farther out on the boom. Involved in making fast the jib's rigging, the lookout suddenly realized that he was working alone. Without a single light to pierce the blackness of the night, he could not figure out what Murray was waiting for. Puzzled he shouted into the blackness, but Murray did not respond. With that he started toward the end of the jib boom and it was only then that the realization hit him that Murray was not responding because he was not there. The *Plover's* worried first mate was simply gone!

For an instant the lookout was in shock and frozen in a near panic. He could not think nor could he act as his mind reeled. Then he instinctively did the only thing that was left for him to do, he made his way back to the deck as fast as he could and ran aft toward the captain's berth shouting at the top of his lungs "Man overboard!" By the time that Captain Jones was awakened and had gained enough of his senses to understand the words of the terrified lookout, most of the rest of the schooner's crew had mustered on deck. Immediately, they began the task of turning the *Plover* about and heading back to attempt to find Murray. The chore of taking a 390 ton schooner and turning it completely around is, however, enormously time consuming. By the time that they had even gotten started in the turn, the *Plover* was already a couple of miles past the place where Murray had been lost. In the open waters of Lake Huron, in the month of April, a person who can swim could expect to survive less than 30 minutes. It took longer than that just to get the *Plover* turned. Once the schooner was turned back, she would now have to tack against the wind in order to work her way back. As if to add to the dilemma, the night was as black as ink and the *Plover* was not equipped with any sort of light that could search beyond the range of a simple oil lamp. There was no marker, or reference of any sort to show where Murray had gone into the water or even if the *Plover* was being guided in his general direction. The lake was an endless black distance across which no one on the little schooner could reach, and out in it was Frank Murray.

By dawn the following day, it was clear to everyone aboard the *Plover* that they would have to give up their search. Hollow-eyed crewmen grudgingly left their positions in the schooner's rigging as Captain Jones set her back up on the downbound course. There had been nothing in sight but miles of choppy water and now it was time to say that Frank Murray had been lost at sea. Indeed, his nightmare had come true and his corpse was now drifting out there among the waves.

Once the *Plover* was back on her course, Captain Jones took the time to go forward and examine the rigging from which Murray had fallen. There was not one broken line, not one loose knot, nothing at all that could cause any man to fall, let alone an experienced sailor. The lookout was questioned at length and said the he had heard not so much as a whimper from Murray. There was no cry for help, no splashing, nothing–Murray had simply gone away. It was almost as if the lake had reached out and taken him away. For the rest of the passage to Detroit, Captain Jones pondered the events surrounding the loss of his first mate. Perhaps Murray had jumped into the lake and committed suicide. Yet, when he had spoken to the captain about his dream, his concern had been for the *Plover* and her crew and for his own family back home, but not for himself. He was not fixating on his own destruction, but on the possibility that something evil was about to happen to those around him, and that hardly sounded like the train of thought of a man bent on suicide. It was only after Murray's loss that the captain confided in his crew and told them of the first mate's dream. Even the most superstitious of the crew would logically conclude that Murray's premonition thus played itself out and the hoodoo was now gone from the *Plover* and her crew. Surely the rest of the season could now be conducted without any ill luck.

Exactly six months after Lake Huron had reached out and taken Frank Murray from the *Plover*, that same vessel was now firmly in the grip of a nasty Lake Superior gale. With her cargo hold stuffed with 18,000 bushels of grain, the schooner had left Duluth on October 7th and had been fighting against opposing winds for two full days. By October 9th, she still had

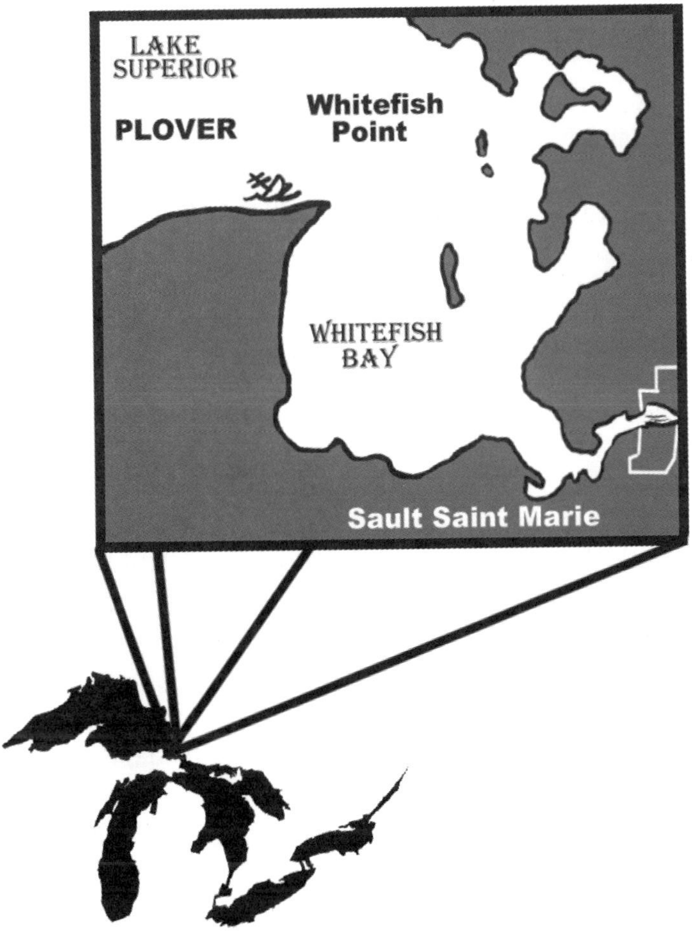

three more days of torment to go before Superior would tire of her and cast her into ruin. Onboard was Captain Jones and a crew of eight sailors including a new first mate who had replaced Murray. Through five frustrating days they fought their way across the big lake, without sleep, without heat and without the choice of surrender. Finally, as they came within reach of the safety of Whitefish Point, they were shoved into the point by the enraged sea. Smashing onto a sand bar, the old *Plover* began to rapidly break up. With that her crew took to her yawl and abandoned the old boat to her doom. By way of lots of rowing, lots of bailing and lots of praying, the nine castaways all made it safely to the sands of Whitefish Point. For the next two days, the crew of the *Plover* hiked toward Sault Saint Marie along a rugged shoreline whose bordering woods were populated with bears that would find any or all of the crew to be a tasty snack. Nothing could be worse than to survive a Lake Superior shipwreck only to be eaten on your way to civilization. They all made it to the Soo, uneaten and thinking of Murray's hoodoo.

Today, the wreck of the *Plover* rests buried in the shifting sands off of Whitefish Point. The shore along which the survivors hiked is nearly as uncivilized as it was in 1871, with the exception of the vacation cottages and the massive Indian casino and hotel that those castaways could not even have dreamed of. Still, when looking out of the hotel's windows toward the shore of Whitefish Bay, we can not only imagine their fears of being eaten by a bear, but also how many times they ran through their minds the thought of that dream of evil things to come that Frank Murray had at the beginning of the season. Indeed, Frank Murray, whose body remains to this day somewhere deep in Lake Huron's eternally refrigerated morgue, had seen his own fate and perhaps that of his boat. No doubt that when Captain Jones and his band of shivering survivors reached the warmth of the Soo, they all felt as if they had somehow escaped Murray's nightmare. Now all that they needed to do is get a lift down the lakes before winter, or they would all be residing in the frozen Soo until next season.

Almost Ghosts

Around America there are states that can claim ghost towns where communities were established, used and then abandoned as soon as the industry that sparked their development was exhausted. From the empty towns of the gold rush to the abandoned pads at Cape Canaveral, every corner of America seems to have its ghost structures. The Great Lakes region is no exception to this rule. Throughout upper Michigan there were plenty of ghost towns left behind at the end of the copper rush as well as at the end of the lumber boom. The lakes, however, can claim distinction for having another type of ghost community and those are the "almost ghost towns." These are the communities that still have a thriving population, but that same population finds itself having been abandoned by the industry that once boomed there. Additionally, the lakes can claim a number of "almost" ghost ships. These are the vessels that have also been abandoned by the mainstream shipping industry and are now left to wait idle at back water docks in overlooked waterways or have been simply designated as a "dead boat" and now serve as storage hulls. On occasion, these almost ghosts can be found in the same locations having been placed there by similar circumstances of fate. In this story you will be taken on a tour of such a place and such a boat. It is presented here, because it is a tour that you would not be able to take yourself.

Driving through Superior, Wisconsin it seems a proper place for a ghost ship to reside. Located at the western tip of

Lake Superior, the city of Superior seems to have benefited the least from the boom in the mid 20th century boom in steel and then suffered the most when the American steel industry collapsed in the 1980s. Around the town are the reminders of the area's glory days of the late 1800s. Buildings and homes can be found, some boarded up and abandoned and others surviving having been altered from their original purpose.

Most apparent Great Lakes ghosts in the city of Superior are the massive abandoned Great Northern ore docks and the Northern Pacific ore dock. These huge docks alone are a study in the evolution of the Great Lakes iron ore industry as they loom from the shore. Each dock is a half mile long and stands 80 feet tall. These docks were designed to feed natural ore by

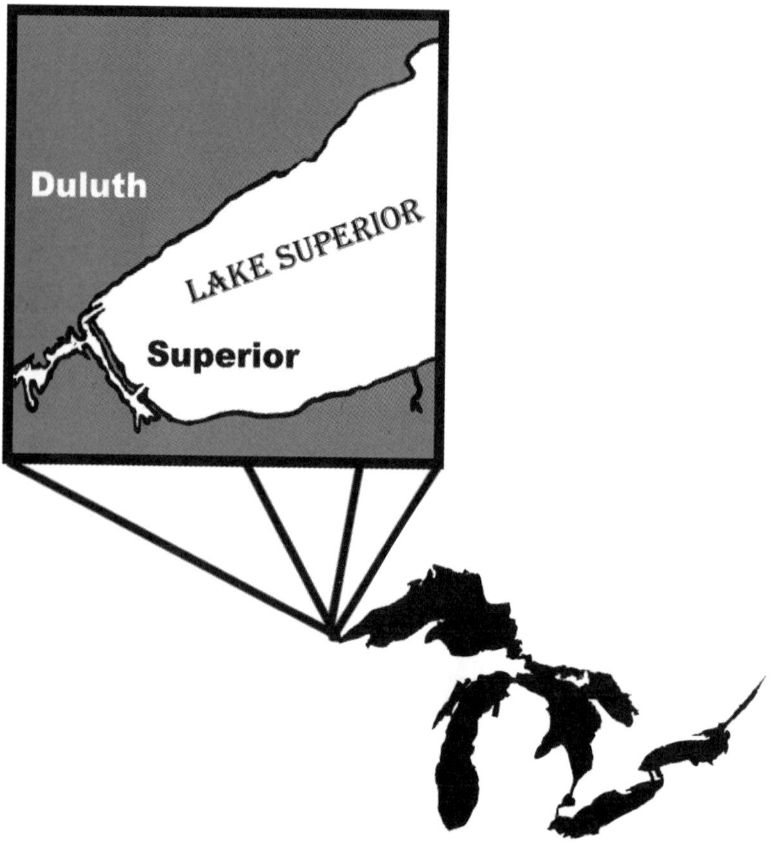

The Northern Pacific ore dock in Superior, Wisconsin.
Author's photo.

gravity into the holds of the big lakeboats. Iron ore is amazingly dense and so a single train load of it is very difficult to move up high enough to then be gravity fed into a vessel. For that reason, wooden trestles lead from the docks and form an inclined plain that reaches several miles through the city. Atop each dock there is room enough to allow four trains to stand on it side by side. The ore was dropped through the bottoms of the hopper cars and allowed to fall into the storage pockets of the dock. Laborers were employed to use long steel poles and while standing on top of the rail cars shove the ore as it was being emptied from the cars and cause it to flow more freely. Each ore pocket on each dock can hold a total of 327 tons of iron ore. The ore would slide down chutes that were lowered into a boat's hold, each pocket having its own chute. When the docks were active, a lakeboat would simply tie up beneath the chutes and the ore would flow in as fast as gravity could pull it. "Natural" iron ore looks very much like red rock and has a high degree of moisture in it. Its moisture content would often cause problems in loading during the late

The early portion of the Northern Pacific ore dock showing the huge iron loading pockets. Author's photo.

shipping season. Temperatures in the Lake Superior region would often drop below freezing in the early autumn and the result would eventually be that the ore would freeze in the pockets while waiting to be loaded. This problem was solved with the advent of taconite pellets. These pellets consist of low grade iron ore that is ground into a fine powder and then formed into marble sized pellets which are then kilned like pottery. This material is far easier to handle and ship than natural ore. There is practically no residual moisture in taconite and so it does no freeze in the pockets and can easily be shipped year round if needed. Also, there was no longer a need to employ dozens of laborers to shove the ore. Taconite simply flowed like marbles and was easily dumped from the hopper cars. The advent of taconite and the construction of a new taconite loading dock to the south of the old ore docks combined with the decline in the American steel industry spelled the end for the giant ore docks.

As the 1980s began, the steel industry was beginning to exclusively use taconite as its ore of choice. Additionally, the new super lakers were showing up in greater numbers. This class of vessel was dominated by the 1000-footers and with their beams of 105 feet they would not fit into the slips of the old docks. Also, it would take over 172 pockets to fill a single 1000-foot lakeboat. The old docks at Superior were suddenly outdated and were subsequently abandoned. Only the most plucky of trespassers venture onto these old docks and to prevent you, the reader, from having to make such a trip the following description is offered.

Standing on the outer edge of the lower pier Northern Pacific dock, the first thing that you notice is how narrow the cement wharf that runs around the dock seems to be. That, however is the only thing about these docks that can be considered small. The pillars upon which the dock stands run along each side of the structure and tower overhead. These pillars are three feet wide and 12 feet thick and are made of stacked concrete forms that are each about one foot tall. The open legs of these pillars are over 40 feet tall and all of the pillars are spaced on 12-foot centers. The footing of each pillar is a an elongated half pyramid of formed concrete that extends

The view looking down the length of the Northern Pacific ore dock. Author's photo.

Satellite photo of the ore docks at Superior, Wisconsin. U.S. Geological Survey.

down more than six feet. Overall the Northern Pacific dock contains more than 350 of these huge pillars. Uniquely, the Northern Pacific dock is divided into two sections. The first third of the dock, which is the section that is the closest to the land, is the "old" original section of the dock and the last two thirds of the structure is the later section of the dock. The difference being that the ore pockets of the old section are huge iron cylinders that are 12 feet in diameter and 25 feet tall. That is about the size of a steam locomotive tipped up on end. There are 51 of these huge pockets on each side of the Northern Pacific dock's old section. The new section is a solid wall of formed concrete that stands just over 30 feet tall. At its base and directly adjacent to each pillar is the opening through which the ore was poured into the chutes. Although some of the chutes still remain on the old Burlington Northern docks, all of the chutes have been removed from the Northern Pacific dock. Between the pillars the inside of the dock is roofed by the cement underside of the ore pockets. These pockets are angled to allow the ore within to slide, so when looking up at the underside of the dock the appearance is that of a huge cement cathedral with a 70-foot high peak. This cathedral-like tunnel runs for a distance of nearly a half mile. Looking closely, it can be seen that the floor of the dock is a carpet of spilled iron ore. In a single sweep of the hand, several different grades of ore can be scooped up. Exploring a bit farther, an area where the weather has washed out some of the spilled ore gives a good indication of just how much iron ore was shipped from this dock over the last century. Here it can be seen that the carpet of spilled ore is over three feet thick! This means that so much iron ore was shipped from this dock that the spillage alone makes up a layer on the dock that is three feet thick. No doubt that a geology buff could take a core sample here and from it watch as the grades of iron ore that were mined this region have changed over the last century.

No one in their proper state of mind attempts to climb atop these docks. Their upper walking surfaces were made mostly

Here the carpet of ore has been washed out of the Northern Pacific ore dock to a depth of 3 feet. The pillar footings can be seen. Author's photo.

of wood and that material has either been exposed to the elements and weakened or been removed by the dock owners. One wrong step could lead to fall to the death for a careless trespasser. The problem that the city of Superior faces with these old ore docks is what to do with these abandoned monster structures? They are so big and built so strongly that they can stand where they are for centuries. If the community decided to try and demolish these structures, the removal of the massive amount of rubble left behind would be outrageously expensive. As of this writing, no one has come up with an answer to this problem and the least costly thing that can be done is to simply leave the old ore docks standing as they are. Thus they remain as abandoned cathedrals to the industrial revolution. They are the places where the ghosts of the Great Lakes shipping industry come to play.

Not far from the abandoned ore docks there rests a ghost ship in waiting. As you drive northward through the city of Superior on Route 2, a glance toward the harbor will likely find a modest off-white painted lakeboat moored at the foot of the LaFarge cement elevators. A closer look will find that she is a bit rusted and her paint is faded and flaking. Her rounded

When she came out in 1904, the Edwin F. Holmes, *later the* J.B. Ford *was typical of the new steel steamers of that era.*
Great Lakes Marine Collection of the Milwaukee Public Library/Wisconsin Marine Historical Society.

Texas deck and tall steamer smokestack seem quite out of place along the Superior waterfront. Even the least observant of boat watchers can tell that this is a very old laker. Painted on her bow in generic lettering is her name–*J.B. Ford.*

Constructed in 1904 the *Ford* originally sailed as the *Edwin F. Holmes* and was part of the class of lakeboats known as the "440 footers." She was the type of oreboat that was specifically designed to load at giant ore docks like Superior's Northern Pacific. Her hatches were deliberately located on 24 foot centers. This feature allowed every other ore chute on the dock to extend and pour through her hatches. Her beam of 50 feet also allowed her to fit handily into the slips between the docks even when other boats were already tied up and loading. In her career as an oreboat she probably visited the Northern Pacific dock many times and the Burlington Northern dock many more times. By the mid 1950s, however, her career as an ore carrier came to an end. The 440 footers were rapidly being outclassed by the bigger boats many of which were now coming out in the 730-foot range. Having run under the name of *E.C. Collins* in Kinsman Marine Transit colors since 1916, she was saved from the scrap yard by the Huron Cement Company in January of 1956. Having her hatches removed, her deck openings welded shut and a hopper unloading system installed she appeared on the lakes as a self-unloading cement carrier in 1959. She operated in that role until November 15, 1985 when she was laid up. In 1989 her five year inspection expired and her owners decided that it was not worth the expense to have her reinspected. Her role was subsequently changed to that of a storage and transfer barge. Although none of her workings were removed, the *Ford* waited in ordinary at the port of South Chicago, unnoticed in the backwaters. When the Huron Cement Company was absorbed into the LaFarge Cement Company, the *Ford* went along with the rest of the Huron assets. No one at the huge international firm of LaFarge really took much notice of her until there developed a pressing need for additional storage capacity at their Superior, Wisconsin facility. In the spring of 2001 the *Ford* was towed as a "dead boat" from her dock in South Chicago and moved to her new home in Superior. Now she remains there, almost a ghost ship as flocks of boat nuts around the lakes wonder what she's like inside. Of course, since you are reading this story, I can take you aboard the old *J.B. Ford* and save you the trip to Superior.

As you climb aboard the *Ford* the first thing that catches your attention is the clutter of secondary equipment that is now fastened to her deck. Everywhere that you look there are the additional pipes and power augmentation needed to make the powdered cement flow through and into her hull. Heading toward her bow, you are naturally drawn to her forward cabins. Standing proudly at her bow, the *Ford's* old-style circular pilothouse and deckhouse echo a bygone era in

Looking through the windows of the J.B. Ford. *All of her equipment remains in place, except for her wheel, which has been removed.* *Author's photo.*

lakeboats which has been all but lost over the years in countless scrap tows. Inside of her pilothouse most of her equipment is intact with one obvious exception–her wheel. Apparently, someone has taken the boat's steering wheel as a souvenir. Aft of her pilothouse an addition was constructed in the mid 1970s to act as her map room. Built of simple plywood, this map room gives you the impression that one good wave would carry it away along with everyone in it. Below the pilothouse in the circular cabin that was her original 1904 wheelhouse, this entire room is reserved for her barrel-sized gyro-compass, which remains in place. Here, the original beauty of the cabin's woodwork is covered with a thick coating of "Huron Cement off-white" paint, which is the same color as the boat's hull. Everywhere that you look on this boat, there is a dusting of cement powder, reminding you of the boat's present day purpose.

Aft of the gyro room in the Texas house are the captain's quarters. Here you see for the first time an unmasked example

Captain's sleeping area on the J.B. Ford. *Notice the fine woodwork. Author's photo.*

Seen here early in her career as Edwin F. Holmes, *the* J.B. Ford *shows her "half-raised" fo'c'sle. Great Lakes Marine Collection of the Milwaukee Public Library/Wisconsin Marine Historical Society.*

of the boat's original woodwork. The walls are paneled in rich oak with a decorative crown-molding running along the entire ceiling. Where the frames exist for all of her original square windows, steel portholes have now been installed. For a long moment you are compelled to pause and admire the beauty of this woodwork. It is a type of expert craftsmanship that was placed into the making of a lakeboat in 1904. There is a pride here and you have to look very carefully to find any flaw.

When the *Ford* was constructed in 1904 it was the trend to make a laker's fo'c'sle deck "half raised" rather than the same height as the other deck houses. This was supposed to keep her profile low and allow for better maneuvering under the loading and unloading docks. Although abandoned by 1908, the half-raised fo'c'sle concept was used in the design of the *Ford*. Thus when you enter the boat's fo'c'sle, you have to descend down a short set of stairs. As you make your way to the *Ford's* starboard companionway door and open it to descend into her fo'c'sle a stunning sight appears. It is an ornate wooden banister that leads down into the companionway. This single item appears to be part of her original woodwork. Dusted in cement powder and showing 97 years of wear, this banister beckons as if to lead you all the way back to the year 1904. On the wall behind the banister is an old ship's telephone, standing by, waiting to be used by a crewman who will never come. At the bottom of the stairs is a classic wooden screen door and beyond it are her cabins. The fo'c'sle is the place where, traditionally, the vessel's mates, wheelsmen and watchmen were quartered. On the *Ford's* starboard side are the rooms for her mates and on the port side are the rooms intended for her non-licensed pilothouse crew. The cabins themselves give us a good lesson in how the sailors of the early twentieth century lived. With the exception of the mate's cabin and guest cabin both of which have double bunks and are equipped with a single sink basin, the other cabins are

Original banister from 1904, leads down into the forward living quarters of the J.B. Ford. *Author's photo.*

J.B. Ford's *officer's galley. Author's photo.*

furnished with triple bunks. Here you get the chance to think of crew being housed, two and three at a time, in these closet-sized rooms for eight months out of the year. There is a community shower at the far end of the companionway on the inboard side where those same crewmen kept clean. Through the door at the end of the companionway is the *Ford's* windlass room. Here is located the gear for moving her huge anchors. She has two different types of anchor chain hawspipes as her starboard anchor is a traditional lakes external and her port side is a modern recessed anchor. At her forepeak an interesting bit of damage is seen. Her forward most deck stanchion has been ripped from the deck at its base and is bent forward toward her towing hawspipe. At the base of the stanchion you can clearly see the marks of a steel cable that had apparently been wrapped around the bottom of the stanchion. It looks as if someone tried to pull her and used the stanchion rather than the towing bits to do so. That careless effort must have ripped the stanchion loose and bent it forward. Other than that single bent stanchion, the entire windlass is in working order.

Entering the port side companionway that leads from the *Ford's* windlass room there is dark passageway on the outboard side. This little passageway leads to what is easily the creepiest place on this old boat–her chain locker and bow peak. There are no working lights in this part of the old boat and exploring here is much like exploring a cavern. The only source of illumination is that which you carry into the room with you, such as a flashlight. If your light goes out, it would be easy to find yourself lost and confused. The chain locker deck, where the boat's anchor chains are piled in two huge steel bins, is a space that is only half a deck high. Walking around in this area requires crouching and the places where you can hit your head are numerous. Then by descending another stairway and going below the chain locker you enter her cavern-like forepeak. Here her bracing and construction stanchions are visible and the thought comes to mind that here is a lot of wasted empty space. Of course the most troubling realization is that there are several hundred tons of anchor chain that are now directly above your head, one deck up, supported by steel that was constructed 97 years ago! Although the *Ford* is sound of hull, you still feel better when you climb out of this area.

Leaving her bow cabins and walking along the *Ford's* spar deck, there is no evidence of her original hatches. Now her hold is accessible by way of a few man holes and just over 60 cylindrical loading scuttles. These scuttles are little more than pipes with steel caps through which the powdered cement is loaded. Other than the man holes and scuttles, the boat's deck is a sealed structure. Below the deck her hold is equipped with a screw-like auger arrangement that runs the length of the hold along her keel and moves the cement powder to the unloading equipment. All of her cargo is moved by means of auger and air. Near the after end of the spar deck there is one clear mark of her earlier days–that is the outline of where her "doghouse" deck cabin once was located before she was converted into a cement carrier. The outline of the base of this deckhouse can be clearly traced on her present deck plating. This cabin was cut away when the boat was converted by the Christy Corporation in Sturgeon Bay.

Reaching the *Ford's* after cabin, entry is gained by way of an access door located in the middle of the bulkhead. The stairway leads down past her oil fuel tanks. A short stroll along the catwalk leads past her auxiliary power equipment and to the boat's heart–her triple expansion steam engine. Some sources say that this is her original 1904 engine, but the Shipmaster's Association Directory from 1948 lists this power plant as having been built in 1927, some 23 years after the vessel was launched. Looking at the engine today, there is no conclusive evidence of the date of construction. The engine can produce 1,400 horsepower using cylinders with diameters of 22-, 35- and 58-inches with a 40-inch stroke. Lubricant still seeps from the bearings showing countless hours of dedication by the countless sailors who served as her oilers. That, however, is the only accumulation of oil found anywhere in the engine room as everywhere else the seals are tight and not

Engine room and engineer's desk aboard the J.B. Ford. *Author's photo.*

even a hint of fuel oil can be smelled. The engine itself is a far cry from any that you may see on display at a museum. The cylinder casing is painted a bland red color and assorted placards are simply penned on it with a felt-tipped marker. The ornate engine gauges that you would expect to see have been replaced by modern gauges and there is no form of decorative scrolling on any of the components or piping. Rather, Huron Cement off-white paint and dull red paint is slopped around the engine and its housing. The engine room itself is a heavily cluttered workspace that more resembles the area of a second rate automotive repair garage than it does the orderly domain of engineers at sea. As if to add to the filth, there is a coating of dirty cement dust on top of everything, and again you are reminded that this is a dead boat and not a powered sailing vessel. Still, some of those who now work with the *Ford* state flatly that her engine equipment could actually be readied to operational condition in a matter of days.

Descending to the base of her engine, you see the yellow-stripes of her propeller shaft just aft of the bearings. High

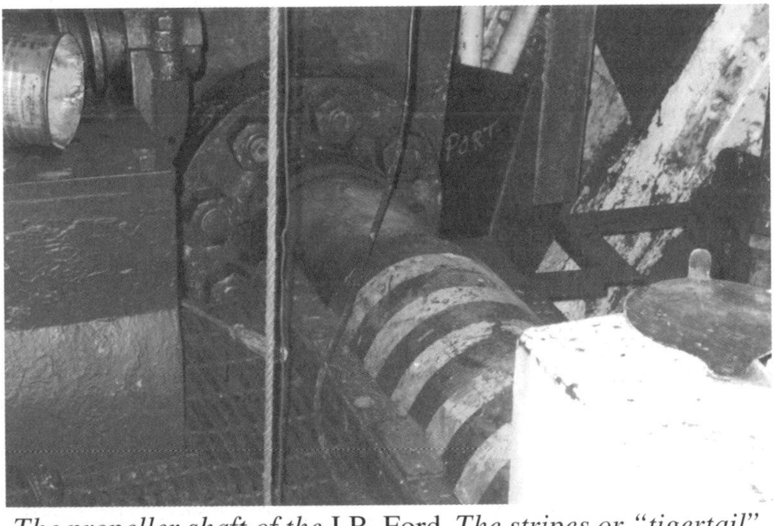

The propeller shaft of the J.B. Ford. *The stripes or "tigertail" is for safety. It is meant to show when the shaft is turning so as to prevent people from being tangled in it.* Author's photo.

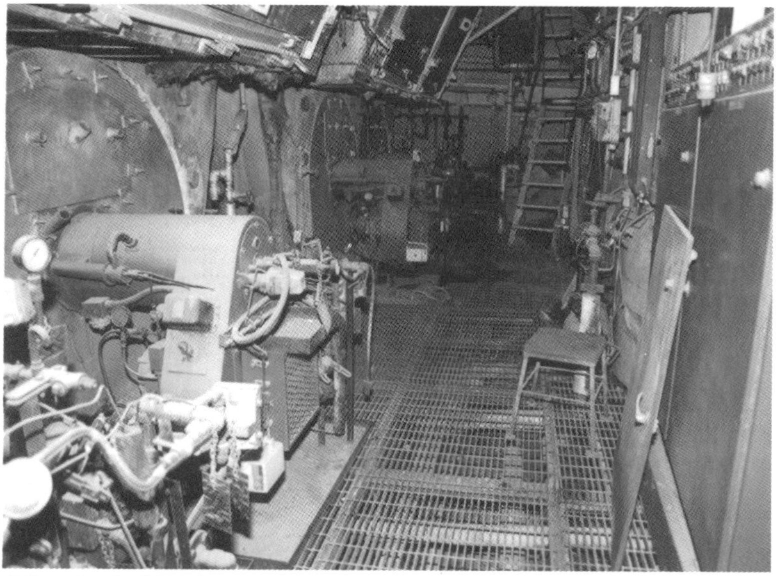

The firehold of the steamer J.B. Ford. *At one time, stokers stood here and shoveled coal into the boilers at the left. Now they are auto-fed oil for fuel.* Author's photo.

overhead, her engine room skylight looms four stories above the base of her engine, which itself stands nearly three decks tall. At the lower level of the engine room, there is a space between her boilers and it is possible to cut through and get to the boat's firehold. Having been converted to burn oil, this area is now far cleaner than in her coal burning days. Lines from the oil tanks feed directly into the boiler furnaces through the doors that her stokers once opened to toss in shovels full of coal. Standing in this area it is not hard to imagine those days when fires licked from the boilers, temperatures hovered over 100 degrees and stokers worked hard at shoveling the coal fuel. In many areas around the engine room, the shipyard workers who did her conversion work in 1959 have used welding equipment to scroll their names and messages in welding beads on areas of the *Ford's* steel structure. Just another way in which she is unique.

Returning to the upper levels of the *J.B. Ford*, you find her upper cabins in a state of abandoned chaos. All of her crew cabins are strewn with discarded clothing, magazines, posters and tools. In sharp contrast to this disorder, her galley has somehow retained much of its natural neatness. As if the spirit of the hundreds of cooks and porters who took so much pride in their work and in the display of her galley have somehow prevented the forces of abandonment from spreading into this area–the galley remains quite orderly. A giant mixer is poised in its storage location on one wall, the stoves are clear of junk and in all of the cupboards dishes, glasses, cups and silverware remain neatly stowed as if waiting to serve a crew, who are forever gone, and a meal that will never be prepared.

In the aftermost part of the stern cabin is the officer's lounge. Like the captain's quarters up forward, this cabin has its original woodwork intact. The image here is one of pure craftsmanship, the likes of which is rarely seen today. Hand-fit crown molding still reflects the pride with which it was installed in 1904. When thinking of the *Ford's* ultimate future and eventual date with the scrap yard, there is sadness in the

The cook's domain of the J.B. Ford. *Author's photo.*

Bow of the J.B. Ford. *Author's photo.*

reality that the yard that scraps this boat, as with so many other old lakeboats, will simply set fire to this woodwork to more efficiently clear it from the steel.

On the *Ford's* fantail our tour ends. Her stack is absent of most of its company colors and has been painted black. On her fantail bulwarks, her towing hawspipe has a reinforced cast iron sleeve, and stamped into this sleeve is the name *"E.C. Collins"* which was the vessel's moniker from 1916 to 1959. From this part of the boat it is easy to look aft and imagine one of the Pittsburgh fleet's huge steel barges at the end of a thick steel towing hawser. At the same time it is hard to keep from wondering how many tons of ore and coal this hull carried in her career before becoming a cement boat.

As you finish our tour, you have the impression that the *J.B. Ford* was happy to have your attention and recognition of her value as a historic artifact–even if that recognition was temporary. As you prepare to leave, the cement carrier *Alpena* comes silently sliding up along side the *Ford*. She is here to unload tons of cement powder and allow the *Ford* to perform the duty that is now her useful existence–storage and transfer. Although the folks at LaFarge Cement fully recognize and appreciate the historic significance of the vessels in their fleet, business is business, and the *Ford* will remain afloat and out of the scrap yard as long as she is a useful asset to the company. Estimates are that the *J.B. Ford* will serve in her current role until about 2010, barring unforeseen circumstances. The reality is that not every old laker can become a museum ship and when the time comes, the most economically responsible disposition of excess tonnage is to sell it for scrap. For now, the old *J.B. Ford* rests in her old age feeling useful, if only as a storage hull. Within her are the fixtures of Great Lakes sailing from another era–she is an "almost" ghost ship. She holds the memories and atmosphere of the golden age of the lakes maritime industry. Just like the city of Superior where she now resides, her heyday has long since past. And just like the people who reside in that city, she is sturdy and not about to let the economics of the maritime industry get her down. They are a good trio, the *Ford*, the Northern Pacific dock and the town of Superior, Wisconsin. They will never lose their heritage, never be toppled by time and always be proud.

Calls To Duty

Often the long months of winter jealously guard their hold on the Great Lakes and when summer finally does begin to edge its way into prominence, winter fights back with gales of wind that would cause November to feel envious. Such was the case in late May of 1889. The spring sailing season had gotten a good start on the fresh water seas and hundreds of vessels of every sort were going about their toil and earning a living by hauling cargoes from one port to another. On Lake Huron, the gray winter ice had turned to shimmering blue water that reflected the color of the bright spring sky. Still the temperatures of that indigo expanse were nearly cold enough to allow the ice to return. From his command at the Sand Beach Life Saving Station, Keeper Plough watched as long lines of lakeboats moved slowly along the horizon like a parade of snails. It was the last week of May, and soon the lake's hazard would turn from spring gales to June fog.

Known in modern times as the town of Harbor Beach, the port of refuge of Sand Beach is located near the tip of Michigan's thumb and in the era of the wooden ship it was often the place where ships and mariners fled in order to escape Lake Huron's rage. Sand Beach was the last shelter for the vessels headed upbound and the first shelter for those headed downbound and passing it by in a gale could mean sailing away into Great Lakes lore as one of those many vessels that simply went missing. For that reason, the port often saw vessels that were badly battered, struggle to make their way through the breakwall. Under those circumstances, vessel captains were often forced to make hard decisions such as abandoning their tow barges outside the harbor in order to limp into port. Others simply ran out of luck and wrecked just outside of the breakwater. All of this made the Sand Beach Life Saving Station one of the busiest on the lakes and Keeper Plough's gaze toward the vessels on the horizon was not one of admiration, but one of expectation. He knew that out there somewhere was his station's next call to duty. In the previous season the Sand Beach station had been called into action on six occasions and had officially been credited with the saving of 53 lives. Keeper Plough had no reason to think that the 1889 season would be any different.

Already in the season of 1889 the storm warriors of the Sand Beach station had been called into action once and had tallied another seven lives saved. Of course that was more of a technicality on paper than it had been an actual rescue. The fact was that the schooner *George C. Finney* had been upbound with a cargo of coal from Buffalo on May 7th when she happened into the jurisdiction of the Sand Beach station. She had hove in too close to the shore and ran onto Elm Creek Reef about seven miles south of the Sand Beach Life Saving Station. There the 301 ton schooner was stuck like a buggy in a bog and nothing that her crew did appeared to be able to get her free. Her master decided to take to the yawl and his crew and row up to Sand Beach to get help from the lifesavers. Of course, it would be just as easy to go there and charter a tug to pull the boat off, but tugs charge fees for that sort of thing, the life-savers however, were government employees sworn to respond to all requests for help and they did so at no cost to the vessel owner. The other side to that coin was that when a crew came calling for help at the lifesaving station, the lifesavers got to tally all of the crew members as "Lives Saved" in their annual report–regardless of the circumstances. Thus when Captain

Riordan and his crew of six landed their yawl at the Sand Beach station at midnight and knocked on the door requesting assistance with their grounded vessel, Keeper Plough and his crew were obliged to help. They were also obliged to place the names of all of the *Finney's* crew into their log as having just been saved. In this not so dramatic action of lifesaving, Keeper Plough escorted the castaways to a local hotel and had them checked in for the night. The following morning the lifesavers took their surfboat and rowed to the *Finney* with her crew and their yawl boat in tow. Unfortunately for Captain Riordan, the schooner had been leaking all night long and it now appeared as if he would have to open his cash box and hire a tug with steam pumps to rid the schooner of the water. Still, for Keeper Plough's lifesavers this was not going to be an easy rescue. In order to get the boat refloated she would have to be lightened of some of her cargo. Working with shovels, the lifesavers and the *Finney's* crew combined to toss overboard a reported total of 50 tons of coal in 32 hours. If you do the math, that equates to over one and one half tons of coal per hour, all of which was shoveled by hand! Eventually, the *Finney* was refloated, repaired and went on to finish her trip. Keeper Plough's crew had gotten their first tally of lives saved for the 1889 season and the only danger that had been experienced was that of blisters from shoveling. Their next call to duty, however, would not be so casual.

While Keeper Plough was pondering the coming of June's fog, his next call to action was getting underway 155 miles to the east over on Georgian Bay. There in the port city of Midland, Ontario the 320 ton schooner-barge *Victor* was topping off a tall deck load of Canadian lumber that was destined to Buffalo, New York. Under the close supervision of Captain Silversides was both the cargo and his 12 year old daughter Minnie. To Captain Silversides the two most important things in the world were his boat and little Minnie and not necessarily in that order. To Minnie, the captain was simply "Papa" and the *Victor* was where he worked and where she lived when she was sailing with him. She saw her Papa as the most sturdy of men and a tower of strength and comfort. Indeed the thought of losing her Papa to any power on earth, be it man or lake, never crossed her mind.

The schooner-barge *Victor* itself was by no means the most sturdy vessel on the lakes. Built in 1867 at Port Dalhousie, Ontario, the once proud sailing vessel had seen better days. Now she was spending her senior years being routinely overloaded and hauling lumber at the end of a towing hawser. For this trip, the *Victor* would be making her trip at the convenience of the steamer *C.W. Chamberlain.* Unlike the *Victor*, the *Chamberlain* was in the early years of her career on the lakes. Constructed at Windsor, Ontario in 1881 the staunch lumber hooker was starting her eighth season on the freshwater seas. At 127 feet in length and 321 tons burden, the *Chamberlain* was exactly the right size to navigate the islands and rocky channels of mighty Georgian Bay. She also had enough power to efficiently tow a barge and this was where the *Victor* entered the picture. Together these two boats could haul prized Canadian lumber down to U.S. ports that were hungry for that material. It was a profitable venture as long as the costs were kept down. Such costs included making any sort of extraneous repairs or alterations to either vessel involved in the operation. So it was that the youthful *Chamberlain* and the creaky old *Victor* set out from Midland loaded for Buffalo as the month of May began to expire.

Every life saving station had a mandated schedule of standard training that was to be completed every week while the station was in service. Wednesday was the United States Life Saving Service's scheduled day for training with the international code of signals. This consisted of a series of flags that spelled out assorted messages when waved in or posted in a given order. So it was that on Wednesday, May 29, 1889, Keeper Plough worked with his crew practicing signals. Each of the lifesavers in turn responded to Plough's questions and properly identified and decoded all of the signals. Such indoor training was suited to the prevailing weather outside. A bitter gray day had formed and the wind was coming up. The sky was heavy with clouds that seemed to be ready to drop buckets of rain at any moment. By the time that the day's training session had ended a nasty chop had developed out on the lake and vessels were already beginning to take shelter within the harbor. Everyone knew that the following day, Thursday, was the day for practice with the beach apparatus and Lyle gun. It was the thought that if the winds kept up it would be a good chance to work with the equipment in storm conditions. What no one could know was that Thursday would bring more practice with that beach equipment than anyone expected.

By midday on Thursday the winds had turned into a respectable spring gale that was ripping across most of the central Great Lakes. At Sand Beach harbor a small fleet of assorted vessels were snugly in shelter behind the port's extensive breakwalls. In town, such weather was a boon to local shops and especially the local saloons. Mariners abandoned their anchored boats, rowed their yawl boats ashore and went "up the street" to spend these stormy hours pursuing interests on dry land. Most of the anchored vessels were left with only one or two crewmen aboard to keep watch on the boat. This was the case for the 64 foot long scow-schooner *Eugene*. She had been downbound with lumber from Au Sable, Michigan when the winds and seas came up. Rather than risk his little lakeboat against the lake Captain Potter decided to take the *Eugene* into Sand Beach and anchor in the harbor. Like many of the other boats in Sand Beach harbor that day, the *Eugene's* crew had left her to venture ashore and only one man remained aboard. Of course, he had plenty to do including focusing the marine glass on the life saving station and watching while Keeper Plough's boys conducted their beach drills.

With the boom of the small cannon known as the Lyle gun and a puff of white smoke the bullet-like projectile whizzed through the air trailing the thin shotline. Over the simulated ship's mast the line fell as the lifesavers pretended that they were actually working a shipwreck. Soon the breeches buoy was rigged and a member of the station crew would climb into the contraption. This device was actually little more than a pair of short canvas pants attached to a standard life-ring. Tied to the ring on four sides were a series of ropes that were attached to a wheel and pulley that suspended the whole rig from a rope running overhead. In the process of evacuating survivors from a shipwreck, each castaway would simply step into the buoy's canvas britches and then be transported by rope to dry land. It was an amazing simple, yet effective tool and the lifesavers had turned its use into an art form. Often on holidays the local lifesavers would thrill crowds of onlookers with demonstrations of the breeches buoy. To show how safe the device was, they would usually ask a lady from the crowd

Two wheel beach-cart used in lifesaving operations. Note the Lyle Gun and stuck beneath it, the projectile. Author's photo.

to ride aboard the rig. On this stormy spring day, however, there would be no crowd of onlookers or giggling ladies to ride the breeches buoy. It was raining hard by the time the rig was set and the wind was blowing a bitter cold that seemed to threaten the return of winter. No one was on the practice grounds who did not have to be there. By early afternoon the drill was complete and Keeper Plough's crew had their gear cleaned, stowed and ready for action.

Aboard the *Eugene*, the ship's lone watchman was in the cabin when he felt the boat shifting and heard the wind blowing across the boat. This was odd since the boat's anchor should have been holding her head to the wind. It only took a moment before he realized what had happened, the *Eugene's* anchor had let go and now the boat was being blown across the harbor. There is little doubt that there was a good deal of scrambling on the part of the watchman to deploy the vessel's other anchor, but such was not a task designed for a single pair of hands. The anchor was big and heavy and by the time the luckless watchman had gotten started at the chore the wind had blown the *Eugene* aground about a half mile south of the life saving station. Having spotted the scow-schooner adrift, the lifesaver on watch rang the alarm and the crew launched their surfboat. It was essentially another drill session as the *Eugene*, although in shallow water, was not in danger of going to pieces. Likewise, the watchman was in no danger of drowning because he could easily wade ashore if he wished. Still, Keeper Plough's crew made haste and soon were at the stranded boat. The watchman requested to be taken off and conveyed ashore and the Sand Beach lifesavers were happy to help. After all, they could then chalk up another "Life Saved" in their station's log. Thus as they returned to the station and began to stow their lifeboat, the Sand Beach crew were in a jolly mood having saved 8 lives so far that season while never having to crest a wave.

As the station's crewman on lookout returned to his post, he immediately began sounding the alarm once again. Staggering into the harbor under her storm sail and sunken down to her rails came the lumber hooker *C.W. Chamberlain.* From the vantage point of the lookout the steamer appeared to be disabled and looked as if she were about to sink at any moment. In moments the storm warriors were at their oars once again and pulling for the wallowing *Chamberlain.* Before they could reach her, however, two small harbor tugs reached the steamer and got lines aboard her. From the steamer's bridge hands beckoned the lifesavers to continue on toward the *Chamberlain.* Once at her side, the Keeper Plough's crew were informed that the beaten steamer had been forced to let go of her barge and now the *Victor* was adrift and helpless out on Lake Huron. It was reported that when last they saw her, the *Victor* was being blown down the lake and toward shore.

While towing the Victor *down Lake Huron, the* C.W. Chamberlain *was overpowered by the winds and waves near Sand Beach. Great Lakes Marine Collection of the Milwaukee Public Library/Wisconsin Marine Historical Society.*

When the schooner-barge disappeared into the rainy distance, she gave every indication that she was sinking.

In modern times, the Coast Guard, which is a direct descendant of the Life Saving Service, has an amazing array of capabilities to locate and rescue vessels in distress. In 1889, however, Keeper Plough had only his savvy and a good horse to rely upon to help in finding the wayward *Victor*. He could have taken his crew and rowed down the lake looking for the lost boat, but what if they had found her in a position that would not allow them to pull along side and rescue the crew? If the beach equipment was needed it would be all the way back up at the station and they would then have to row all the way back to get it. His choice was clear, he would take his crew back to the station and then he alone would ride down the coast to see if he could locate the *Victor*. Darkness was rapidly setting in and to further save time, Keeper Plough ordered his crew to go to the livery stable and get a team of horses to pull both the beach cart and the boat cart down the shore and meet him at the wreck.

Keeper Plough rode as far down as the limit of his crew's night foot patrol, about three miles south of the station. There he used his marine glass to scan the darkness. A dim lamp and the white foam of the breaking waves betrayed the location of the *Victor*. The boat appeared to be about 150 yards off of the beach and was offering no clue as to her condition. Although the temperature of the lake water was not that of April or November, it was still plenty cold and Plough knew that if the boat went to pieces, most or perhaps all of her people were likely to be lost in the surf. Still, all that he could do would be wait until his crew arrived. It would be a long and helpless wait.

Aboard the *Victor* the situation was not good. The old boat had run hard into the shallows–so hard in fact, that her hull had split lengthwise from the impact. All that was holding the old boat together at that point was her deck load of lumber. The mass of the deck load was preventing the two halves of the hull from moving apart and keeping her people out of the lake–for the moment. For little Minnie Silversides, this was a terrifying experience, but she was safely in the protective hug of her papa. Indeed there was little that Captain Silversides and his crew of five could do for the *Victor* at that point. The boat was clearly finished and it was only a matter of time before the lake picked her apart. The four men who made up the crew of able bodied seamen were as helpless as the boat itself. The boats weather rigging had been torn away by the seas and all that anyone could do was to keep a single lantern with a red cloth wrapped around it lighted and swinging in the hope of signaling for help. Down in the galley, the cook, who was a woman of 202 pounds had long since lost her cooking stove's fire to the incoming lake. She had no duty left to perform and her job aboard the *Victor* was at its end.

Amid the despair of the *Victor's* crew there came a bright flare of hope as Keeper Plough set off a Coston signal to let them know that the United States Life Saving Service was on the way. As he waved the handheld flare he was also signaling that the most experienced storm warriors on the Great Lakes, the Sand Beach station crew, were coming to the rescue. By nine o'clock that evening the rest of the crew of the Sand Beach station arrived on the scene and Keeper Plough directed that the beach equipment should be deployed. With the rhythm of men who had practiced this maneuver a hundred times, the crew quickly set out the equipment and prepared the Lyle gun. With the first shot Keeper Plough placed the line directly across the *Victor*. In minutes his well trained crew had the breeches buoy rigged and were running it out to the wreck. Traditionally, a male member of the ship's crew would always be the first to ride the breeches buoy from the wreck to the beach to test the soundness of the rig. That was how it went on the night of the *Victor's* wreck. One of her able bodied crew took the first ride from the wreck and was landed safely on the beach. For reasons that are not recorded, a second able bodied seaman made the next trip. This may have been because Captain Silversides wanted to make absolutely certain that the rig was safe before committing his daughter Minnie to the device. What is recorded was that little Minnie Silversides was the third person to board the breeches buoy. Terrified that she may never again see her papa, the little girl had to have her arms pried from around her father. Sobbing, she was placed into the canvas britches and sent dangling along the hawser toward shore. Below her tiny feet Lake Huron churned like a mad beast snapping toward her waiting to eat her up with its icy jaws of water. She closed her tear filled eyes tightly and sobbed for her papa. The wind howled through the ropes that made up the rig and for a time she was between the shore and the boat, but could see neither. There was only the roar of the lake, the howl of the wind, the sting of the rain and the dark coldness that surrounded her.

A distance of more than a football field's length separated the *Victor* and the Sand Beach lifesavers. As they pulled at the lines that ran the breeches buoy, they could not see Minnie through the darkness. She could be dipping into the seas for all they knew, so the men simply hauled on the line knowing that her life depended on their hands. After what seemed like hours, but was actually just a few minutes, the soaked, cold sobbing little girl appeared from the darkness and in moments she was lifted from the breeches buoy and placed safely in the care of one of the *Victor's* crewmen. As the rain spit and the surf roared, he tried to assure her that her papa would be coming along soon. But he knew too well that he may be telling her a lie. The mast to which they had rigged the breeches buoy had become unstepped when the boat's hull split and all that was holding it in place was the cargo of lumber that had been wedged up against it. Just a little too much pulling on the hawser that held the breeches buoy could easily topple the mast and strand whoever remained aboard the wreck. The wreck itself was rapidly going to pieces and there would surely be no chance to rig another shot before Lake Huron could swallow every human trace that remained on the *Victor*. To make matters worse, the surf was continually shoving the wreck toward shore and causing the hawser line on which the breeches buoy traveled to repeatedly go slack. This forced the lifesavers to retighten the line after each person made the trip and added further delay to the process.

Next to leave the *Victor* was the ship's cook–all two hundred and two pounds of her. As the lifesavers began to pull on the breeches buoy to reel her in they were unable to see what they were hauling because of the darkness. The effort made some wonder if the rig had fouled. As she appeared out of the night, the Sand Beach storm warriors suddenly got a look at the large woman wedged tightly into the rig.

"I feel like we're pullin' the whole boat ashore." One of the lifesavers mumbled.

He was close enough for little Minnie to hear his remark and she smiled in spite of her ordeal. Of course there was real danger in this part of the rescue. The added strain on the hawser could cause it to work loose from the unstepped mast and that could mean the end for everyone else on the wreck. Still the lifesavers tugged on and finally landed the cook safely on the beach. Then they were faced with the difficult chore of removing the cook from the canvas britches. Of course in 1889, ladies of such dimension were considered to be the height of fashion. Thus the cook composed herself and comforted Minnie as some of the lifesavers looked on and wondered if she were single.

Two more of the *Victor's* crew came across in the breeches buoy before the rig came swinging back to pick up Captain Silversides. Taking the rain soaked ropes in his hands, he took one last look at his shattered command. The boat was clearly a total loss and it was likely that most of the cargo would be lost as well. His time aboard the *Victor* was at its end and now all that he had left to do was to escape with his life. Stepping into the canvas britches he hoisted the rig snugly above his waist and stepped from the *Victor* for the last time.

On the beach the lifesavers aided by the *Victor's* crew hauled at the lines as they attempted to pull Minnie's papa to shore. The line tossed and moved as if the *Victor* was entering a tug of war with those who would save Captain Silversides. The lifesavers were skilled, however, and had practiced this routine many times. There was no way that Keeper Plough and his crew were going to lose Minnie's papa to Lake Huron. With a determination not to let the lake beat them, the Sand Beach lifesavers pulled Captain silversides from the darkness and from the icy jaws of an angry Lake Huron. As the good captain's feet hit the sand, the small group who were witnesses to the wreck of the *Victor* broke into applause. It was a small, but genuine celebration of victory.

After a long three and one half mile walk back to the Sand Beach Life Saving Station, lead by Keeper Plough, the castaways from the *Victor* were finally indoors by midnight. Minnie had her papa safely in her arms once again and the crew of the Sand Beach station could add another tally of seven lives saved to their log for the season of 1889.

Today, the harbor of Sand Beach has long since been renamed as Harbor Beach and it is a place alive with its maritime heritage. Each summer there is a three day maritime festival with events ranging from Jet Ski races to parades of classic cars. The lighthouse is well on the road toward loving restoration as the local citizens give their own time to guarding that part of the harbor's history. Unfortunately, no human efforts could do anything to save the old life saving station. Like the original life saving station which was located on land near the center of the harbor, the second station was built on a pier and it is in an advanced state of decay. Officials of the State of Michigan have declared it to be unsaveable and beyond any restoration. Lake Huron has sent so much weather and directed so much anger toward the

This is the "second" Coast Guard Station at Harbor Beach. It has now been abandoned and condemned. Author's photo.

The remains of Harbor Beach's original Life Saving Station. *Author's photo.*

station that it will soon be overcome. Like the *Victor*, whose bones remain in the sands just south of Harbor Beach, the Sand Beach Life Saving Station will soon be swallowed by the waters of Lake Huron. For the record, however, there were many times when the lake did not win and did not claim a human prize. Often those victories resulted from a call to duty and the response of Keeper Plough and his storm warriors of the Sand Beach station. It was because of their professionalism that Minnie Silversides was able to return home in the company of her papa.

Yado

From her home near the lake and harbor of Buffalo, New York, Margaret Mahoney heard the steamer's whistle blowing distress calls. Through the entire night the whistles could be heard blowing from out on Lake Erie in a haunting cry that did not let up. She knew that most of the boats on the lakes were done for the season and thought for sure that the only one due into Buffalo at that moment was the one that her beloved Simon was on. The sounds of the whistle were clearly not the normal signals blown by the harbor tugs, these were the whistles of one of the big lakeboats and it sounded as if it was in trouble. Somehow she knew that it was Simon's boat–she just felt it deep in her soul. In her mind she pictured him doing his best to save his ship and she tried not to think too much about the horror of his drowning in the frigid waters of Lake Erie. The snow and the darkness of the night obscured everything and dropped a black curtain off shore. No one could see beyond a few yards out onto the lake. Then, as suddenly as they had started, the distress signals ended shortly after dawn. Now, as it had been for the last 36 hours, there was only the screaming wind and the pelting snow.

For reasons that are not in any records, the Great Lakes mariners of the late 1800s and early 1900s were in the habit of signing aboard their vessels of employment using assumed names. The reasoning behind such a practice probably has more to do with the individual mariner than with some mass trend toward trying to hide identities. We don't really know why Chief Engineer Simon O'Day preferred to be known to his shipmates as "Yado" which was his name spelled backward, but he often used that moniker in maritime circles. In fact he actually liked it when people called him by that name.

At the close of the 1909 season, Chief Yado was working for the Hutchinson fleet and living in Buffalo. On the seventh day of December Yado and his boat, the 500 foot steel steamer *William A. Paine*, were headed down the St Clair and Detroit rivers bound for Buffalo and a long winter's lay up. The 1909 sailing season on the lakes had been, in terms of casualties, one of the worst since steel lakeboats had come into prominence. So far a total of 71 mariners had perished in the waters of the Great Lakes. This season it seemed that whenever storms were not raking the lakes, fog was smothering them and in among all of that mess the mariners and their vessels had struggled to earn a living. To add to the troubles, the season had started with a turbulent strike by the union that represented the vessel engineers and tensions had run high all season long. Those mariners who saw the season of 1909 end were happy to tie their boats to the dock and go home to wait out the winter months. No doubt that Chief Simon "Yado" O'Day was ready to trade his engine room for his Buffalo address.

His first order of business upon getting into Buffalo would be to call upon his 27-year-old bride to be, Margaret Mahoney. In his writings to her he had predicted that he would be back in Buffalo on or about December 8th and she was expecting his arrival. A date of April 5, 1910 was set to be their wedding day, depending of course, on when Yado was called upon to return to his boat. At age 31, and holding a steady job as a chief engineer aboard a lakeboat, Yado was quite a catch for the young Irish lass. Of course for Yado himself, working on the lakes was sort of a family tradition and making the rank of chief was expected. His father, Simon R. O'Day Sr., had been a vessel man for many years out of Muskegon, Michigan. Unlike his son, the senior O'Day had earned his wages in the pilothouse rather than the engine room. He worked his way up and eventually commanded the vessels *D.W. Powers* and *C. Hickox*. Yado had gotten tired of high school and dropped out to seek his future on the lakes. He started out in the engine room serving in the position of wiper and worked his way up to chief engineer. Exactly how Yado met Margaret Mahoney no one can recall, but the beginnings of their relationship seems a bit tentative. Reportedly he once came calling on her and discovered that she was out on a date with another man. This got the dander of the Irishman up and he decided to make his stand right then and there. He planted himself on the stoop of the Mahoney home and waited. Hours passed but finally Margaret and her date came strolling up the street. As soon as they were in range, Yado strode up, stepped between them and

Seen here in the 1920s era, the William A. Paine *sports a round lower pilothouse. In 1909, she would not have been equipped with the upper pilothouse. Great Lakes Marine Collection of the Milwaukee Public Library/Wisconsin Marine Historical Society.*

began talking to Margaret "...in such a manner as to completely exclude Margaret's date from the conversation." Soon her "date" got the message and he huffed off into the evening, never to be heard from again. From that moment on, Margaret and Yado were a couple. Now all that he needed to do was to get the *Paine* in for the winter and he could concentrate on the lady of his dreams.

As the *Paine* snaked her way down the Detroit River, the winter had clearly taken charge of the Great Lakes. A thick blizzard was blowing and the snow flew horizontally past the lights of the vessel. In the pilothouse of the *Paine*, Captain Detloff was using every bit of his experience as a lake mariner to guide his boat. Each turn that the boat needed to navigate became a problem that was solved more with the instinct of the captain than with the tools of navigation. Down in the engine room, Yado was a world away from the winter blizzard. The atmosphere in the engine room was usually heated to over 100 degrees and the boat's thick steel hull easily blocked any sign of the howling wind. His only concern was the operating condition of his engine and the activity of his engine room crew. So long as they all worked like the well-oiled machine that they were, the *William A. Paine* would reach Buffalo and end her season. Of course that season ending mentality could easily change if management decided that another trip would be needed.

The *Paine* was not alone in her downbound passage through the blizzard. Also feeling her way down the river was the steamer *W.C. Richardson*. Like Captain Detloff on the *Paine*, Captain Enos Burke was using all of his experience to bring the *Richardson* out of the river. Having her hold filled with 200,000 bushels of flaxseed, the *Richardson* was on her way down from Duluth to Buffalo and was expected at the Kellogg elevator at about the same time as the *Paine* was due into that same port. Constructed in 1902, the *Richardson* was just 374 feet in length and was among a series of 300 footers built in that era. She was not designed to make her living hauling massive quantities of ore. Rather she had been designed to be as handy as possible in the carrying of as many different types of cargoes as could be imagined. This theory proved to be sound as a number of these turn of the century 300 footers went on to sail well into the 1960s. In every respect the *Richardson* was a modern and absolutely seaworthy vessel for her day. It did not matter if she were hauling ore, coal or grain, she was as comfortable a boat as anyone could want.

Captain Burke successfully guided the *Richardson's* bow onto an enraged Lake Erie and into the teeth of the gale just before midnight on Monday, December 6, 1909. In close company with the *Richardson* was the *William A. Paine* with Chief Yado doing his best to keep the thousands of tools in his engine room from being scattered by the rolling of the boat. As the night went on what appeared to be a strong winter gale turned into a real monster. Winds actually reached hurricane force as temperatures dropped well below freezing. The water from the crests of the waves was ripped away by the winds and slung against the two lakeboats. As the super-cooled water impacted any part of either vessel it froze instantly. Soon both boats looked more like powered icebergs than vessels. Windows were iced over and doors were frozen shut. Each vessel's steel deck became ice-coated like a skating rink that was slick from the boarding seas. Venturing outside onto the deck would mean certain death for any crewman dumb enough to do so. With the boats rolling and the icy deck, a person would instantly lose their footing and go sliding into the deadly clutches of Lake Erie. Anyone that was in the forward section of the boat when it left the confines of the Detroit River would be forced to remain forward until either the boat reached Buffalo or the storm died. Likewise, anyone who was residing in the after cabins was also stranded there for the duration of the storm. To Yado it was not really a problem. His engine room was aft, as were both his cabin and

Seen here on a fine summer day, the W.C. Richardson *enjoys her third season of operation. Guests crowd her open-air pilothouse as she moves through the Saint Marys River in 1905. Great Lakes Marine Collection of the Milwaukee Public Library/Wisconsin Marine Historical Society.*

the galley. He had a hot engine room, hot food and a warm bed. To him, it was simply another day at work. Likewise, over on the *Richardson* Chief Engineer Samuel E. Mayberry was fairly comfortable in his kingdom of steam. He had checked the boat's tanks and she was not shipping a drop of water. Her cargo was dry and the *Richardson* was running as tight as a drum. He too was wishing that this would be the last trip of the season, but he knew too well that old man Richardson would pile another run on the boat in an effort to squeeze every dollar that he could out of 1909. What the *Richardson's* chief engineer could not know, was that the ice water of Lake Erie would grant him his wish and make this his and the *Richardson's* final trip of the season. His wish, however, would come true in a way that he could not imagine.

Through the entire day Tuesday and into the early morning of Wednesday the *Richardson* and the *Paine* plowed ahead toward Buffalo. Although the gale had been at their heels, the waves presented a constant threat to their steering equipment and the winds continually threatened to blow them around into the trough of the seas. As close a watch as possible was kept on the hatches of both boats. Hatch covers in this era were large wooden planks that were laid side by side across the hatch opening. Canvas tarps were then spread across the hatches and long steel rods were placed over top of the canvas to make the rig water-tight. In a gale such as this, the waves would often pick endlessly at those hatch covers until if found a weakness. The seas would then work as if guided by some evil presence of the lake to exploit that weakness. Once a single tarp had been worked loose, the hatch planks that it had covered would be easy prey. If the crew was unable to reach and repair the weakened hatch cover, the lake would soon peel it open and invade the cargo hold. At the same time, the rest of the seas would work at the other hatches. It was a deadly game that those who ventured onto the lake at the wrong time were forced to play. Using the *Richardson's* big spot light Captain Burke kept sweeping the deck, watching his hatches. In his heart he knew that if any of the hatch covers did pull loose, there was little that he could do about it. The deck was a mass of ice and no one dared to go out onto it. Still, that same ice helped the situation. Acting like a giant cast, it froze the hatches shut and turned the tarps and strongbacks into one solid piece. If the good captain's luck held, they would make Buffalo along with their excess cargo of ice.

In the pilothouse of the *Paine*, the atmosphere was about the same as it was aboard the *Richardson*. In spite of the fact that his boat was three years younger and twice as big as the *Richardson*, Captain Detloff still kept a close eye on his hatches. Both vessels were navigating by compass and clock alone. Given a set number of turns on the propeller, each master calculated his speed and knew the distance and headings required to get from the Detroit River to Buffalo. They had both made that trip hundreds of times and the route was committed to their memory as was their vessel's performance. By mentally figuring in the wind's influence on their boat, each master knew about how long to make the run without running out of lake on the other end. This was a critical skill in the gale of December 1909, because the daylight hours on Tuesday had been filled with blinding snow and the night was as black as tar. There were no land marks and no lighthouses to be seen from the pilothouse of either boat and both masters were running nearly blind. Their only advantage was that it was so late in the season that there were fewer other vessels out there for them to hit.

During the night, both masters checked down their vessel's revolutions to slow down and thus compensate for the wind. Each captain wanted to arrive off of Buffalo in the daylight so as to have a better chance at entering the harbor. Such a check-down was a true gamble. The wind that had grown to hurricane force the previous day was not letting up. If either vessel was to lose too much forward inertia, their stability in the water could be degraded to the point where the wind could take hold of their stern and swing them around into the trough of the sea. This could become a position from which a lakeboat could not recover. The check-down appeared to be well timed, because at four o'clock on Wednesday morning, through a break in the snow, Captain Burke spotted the Point Abino light. He was a little over two hours from Buffalo harbor.

Ashore, the streets of Buffalo were filled with drifted snow as Wednesday morning turned into afternoon. Telegraph lines had been blown down and everyone feared the worst for the few lakeboats that remained out on Erie's churning surface. Their fears were elevated substantially when the sounds of a vessel's whistle frantically blowing distress signals were carried ashore with the wind that evening. The distant, but clear distress call echoed through the streets and bounced off the wooden sides of the homes and then swirled through the air along with the snow. Butchers wiped their hands on their stained aprons as they stepped from their shops to listen. Wagon men held a cupped hand to their ear and elevator workers stepped from the clouds of grain dust to listen. Ladies held their hats with one hand and their collars with another as they squinted into the blowing snow and heard the far away cries. One lady in particular was more attuned to the distress whistles than any one else in the city–Margaret Mahoney. When she heard the whistle blowing its distant cry for assistance, she simply knew it was the *Paine* and that Yado was at the mercy of Lake Erie. The distress whistles continued from early evening and went on right through the entire night.

What the blizzard had blotted out was the true drama that was being played out on the Lake Erie. The *Paine* had arrived off of the Buffalo breakwall and found the seas far too rough to allow her to pass into the harbor. The winds were shifting more to the north and a nasty cross-sea had formed and effectively blocked the entrance. Captain Detloff elected to drop his anchors and wait out on the lake until the weather moderated rather than risk being impaled on the breakwall in a pointless effort to enter the harbor. Around mid-morning the *Richardson* arrived and also found the conditions too rough for entering the harbor. Some sources say that after the *Richardson's* captain made his decision not to make an attempted run into the harbor, he turned his boat, running her back out into the lake. Others say that he simply checked down too far in an attempt to slow his boat and delay approaching the harbor and let her drift. Whatever the reason, the wind got the better of the *Richardson* and the lake used her loss of headway to grab the boat with a huge wave and trap her in the trough of the sea. Before Captain Burke could get up enough power and headway to turn the *Richardson* out of the trough, Lake Erie sent a series of sweeping waves to finish her.

Marching the length of Lake Erie, some 250 miles, and having near hurricane force winds behind them, the waves that attacked the helpless *W.C. Richardson* came in rapid

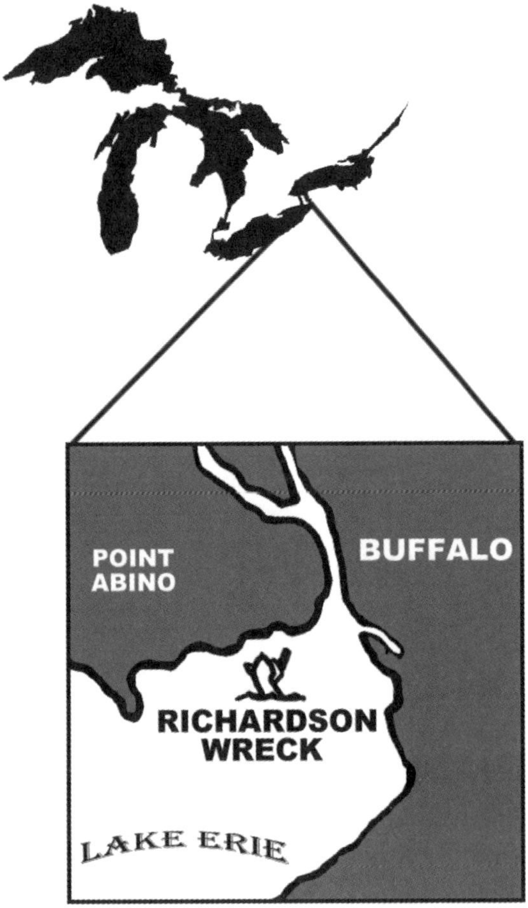

succession. First they swept her deck and then they battered her after cabin. In short order they found the passageway to her engine room and began to cascade in looking to snuff out the fires that kept her alive. Immediately, Captain Burke knew his vessel was in deep trouble. He ordered Chief Mayberry to start blowing distress signals. He figured they were near Waverly Shoal and about six miles from Buffalo harbor. Certainly, someone would hear their signals and come to the rescue.

It did not take long for Lake Erie to overwhelm the *Richardson*. Soon the wind and waves pushed her over on her beam ends and her cargo of flaxseed shifted. Down in the boat's firehold her stokers were trying to keep their footing on the 30 inch wide grated floor while they shoveled coal into the boat's furnaces. As the *Richardson* turned on her beam ends the deck below them canted like steel teeter-totter. Coal from the bunker behind them came rumbling down in a black avalanche. The doors to the boiler furnace tubes flung open while sparks and hot embers swirled in the air. From overhead the roar of a thousand rainstorms echoed as Lake Erie entered the companionway door and cascaded down into the firehold. In an instant it found the boat's fires and snuffed them out filling the engine room with filthy steam. If this was not certain death, it sure looked like it to the engine crew as they clamored to escape. Without her fires, the *Richardson* had no steam, and without steam she was now powerless against Lake Erie.

Now the waves swept the deck and were able to get at the hatch covers that they had desired for so long. With the boat listed over the waves had just the right deck angle to rip away the canvas and smash the hatch planks. Captain Burke ordered the anchors dropped in the hope of bringing the boat's head to the seas. It was a move that was made far too late. The short December daylight was rapidly running out and Wednesday's evening was setting in. Worse yet, the lake had been successful in opening the hatches to the *Richardson's* after hold and the boat was rapidly sinking by her heels. Every scrap of wood that could be gathered was ripped from the after cabins before the stern settled. The crew of the *Richardson* then went forward and built a bonfire as a signal of distress.

From the pilothouse of the *Paine* Captain Detloff saw the fire just long enough through the blizzard to conclude that a vessel was in distress out in the thickening darkness, then a series of snow squalls blotted out everything. Captain Detloff knew that she was a steamer and if she had to use a fire to signal for help it meant that her fires were out. The situation left him in a very awkward and helpless position. If he raised his anchors and went charging to the rescue in the darkness and the blizzard, he could easily either miss the distressed boat or worse he could accidentally run her down. The *Paine* had no wireless radio and so he had no way to communicate with anyone ashore and tell them of the vessel in distress. The port of Buffalo was about three miles away and so the only method that Captain Detloff could use to signal ashore was the *Paine's* steam whistle. With alerting the lifesavers in mind, Captain Detloff began blowing distress signals, and he kept blowing that whistle all night long.

Aboard the *Richardson* the situation was rapidly deteriorating. As the boat's stern settled lower into the lake, the crew trapped there attempted to escape. Forming a human chain, they all made a dash across the icy deck together, and Lake Erie reached out to claim one of them. In the chain of castaways were ship's cook John Branford and his wife and it was them that the lake set its sights upon. Sending a frigid mountain of water, Lake Erie thundered over the side of the *Richardson* just as the human chain was amidships. Slamming down upon them it knocked everyone from their feet, broke their grip upon one another and carried away Mrs. Branford. A single cry was heard as she was taken away and swallowed by the lake. There was no way to help her, and no way to rescue her, she was simply gone.

Once all of the remaining crew were mustered at the *Richardson's* bow, Captain Burke, whose decision making had put them into this situation in the first place, began to concoct another hair-brained scheme. He reckoned that the only way to get assistance was to send the yawl boat ashore with a bunch of men aboard to summon the lifesavers. The term "never volunteer for anything" truly applies here. The wind was blowing at about 50 miles per hour, the air temperature was below freezing and quite likely below zero and the waves measured in the 18 to 20 foot range. As if that were not enough, the water temperature was just above freezing and any human submersed in such cold water could expect to live just a few minutes. Now Captain Burke was asking for volunteers to man a 10 foot long open boat and try to float a half dozen miles to shore. What is even more remarkable is that he actually got four volunteers!

Battered by the waves, the hulk of the Richardson *rests with its bow high and dry. The wreck was later dynamited and cleared to prevent it from remaining a hazard to navigation. Great Lakes Marine Collection of the Milwaukee Public Library/Wisconsin Marine Historical Society.*

"I'll go for one." Second mate E.J. Cleary announced. "Who'll go with me?"

"Well." Chief Mayberry reasoned. "The fires are out, so there's nothin' more for me to do here. I'll go."

"So will I." Said ship's fireman Sidney Smith.

Of course, stupidity loves company and so Ed Gransey volunteered with Smith to round out the crew of the yawl.

In the darkness and the blizzard it was a tough chore to lower the little yawl boat filled with the volunteers, but they were eventually put over the side.

"So long." One of the yawl's crew sang out as they vanished into the darkness surrounding the *W.C. Richardson.*

That was the last that was ever seen or heard from those four volunteers. So far as current research shows, both the yawl boat and its crew of volunteers were never found. It was later speculated that their remains may have been caught in the flow of the Niagara River during the winter and then sent over the falls. No matter what their final disposition may have been, there is one thing that we can say for sure, Chief Mayberry got his wish–this was his last trip, his season was over.

As dawn broke on Thursday the gale was finally beginning to break. From the pilothouse of the *Paine* the wreck of the *Richardson* began to become visible in the dim morning. With binoculars Captain Detloff could see that the boat had sunk to the point where her stern was fully under water. The bow of the *Richardson*, however, was still above the surface of Lake Erie. Each wave that smashed into the bow of the sunken steamer appeared to burst completely over her. Worse yet, there were people moving around on that bow. Captain Detloff knew that there was not a moment to waste. Calling down to the engine room, he told Yado to make steam for full ahead and be ready for plenty of maneuvering, they were on their way to rescue the crew of the *Richardson*.

This effort in rescue would require some extraordinary seamanship. The *Paine* would have to be brought close enough to the wreck for the *Richardson's* crew to escape, yet not collide with the wreck which would likely sink it. Captain Detloff decided to bring his boat up on the leeward side of the wreck and once along side he would drop his anchors. With the anchors keeping the *Paine* in a safe hover near the *Richardson's* bow, he would have Yado make revolutions for slow ahead. As the anchors held the bow and the propeller established rudder effectiveness, Captain Detloff put the wheel over and spun the stern so as to rotate on the anchors. This maneuver brought the *Paine's* bow gently against the wreck.

Without hesitation, the crew of the *Richardson* began leaping to the deck of the *Paine*. Some of the *Paine's* crew lashed ropes between the two boats in an effort to insure that the boats would remain together long enough for all 14 survivors to get to safety. Captain Burke was the last to leave his boat and as soon as Captain Detloff was assured that everyone was safe, the lines between the boats were released, the *Paine's* hooks were cranked up and the boat headed for Buffalo. At eight o'clock Thursday morning the *William A. Paine* entered Buffalo harbor. She was met by the tug *Cascade* and lines were exchanged. Once safely on the end of the tug's line the *Paine* moved to the Great Eastern elevator where her cargo was consigned. The survivors from the *Richardson* were then unloaded onto a launch and whisked away to an undisclosed location on Commercial Street. There they would be kept from the press until the company could debrief them. The end tally for that December gale on Lake Erie added an additional 57 mariners to the 1909 death toll. The *Richardson's* survivors had been lucky to have escaped with little more than frostbite.

One drawback to Captain Detloff's all night blowing of the *Paine's* whistle was that he accomplished exactly what he had set out to do–he alerted the Buffalo lifesavers. Unfortunately, when Keeper William Greisser and his crew of storm warriors deployed on the beach, the distress signals seemed to be coming from far out on the lake. The night was too black and the blizzard was too thick to simply launch their surfboat and pull blindly onto the open lake. They would never be able to find the signaling boat. Of course we know that even if they did manage to home in on the whistles, they would have found the *Paine* and not the *Richardson* anyhow. Their only choice was to wait through the night on the beach and head out at dawn. We can only imagine their frustration as they paced about in the sand and driftwood stoking their bonfire and listening to the deep moans of the that steam whistle calling for the help that they had trained so hard to give. At first light they launched into what remained of the blizzard and pulled at their oars as if to vent the night's frustration. The waves were still running high and each seemed to explode over the lifesavers as they thwarted the lake and headed out. By the time that Keeper Greisser spotted the wreck through the snow, his crew had been covered in ice from the spray. Still the lifesavers pulled ahead determined to rescue anyone who needed them. Oddly, they were the ones in the greatest danger at that moment. Although they had no way of knowing it, the *Paine* had already removed every living soul from the scene. Then as the surfmen drew near the *Richardson* they were met by the tug *W.G. Mason* and the fireboat *William G. Grattan.* The two steamers were on the same mission as the lifesavers and had already visited the abandoned *Richardson.* Informed of the wreck being abandoned, the lifesavers simply turned back. When they reached their station, after having rowed a round trip distance of nearly ten miles, the lifesavers were soaked, exhausted and covered with ice. It was a good thing that this was the end of the season.

As soon as Captain Detloff rang "Finished With Engine" on the pilothouse chadburn, Yado was free to go up the street and finally calm a worried Margaret. They were married the following April and later that year she actually went on a trip with him. We do not have a record as to which of the Hutchinson boats the two of them sailed upon, but we do have a story that has been handed down about their trip. It is said that both Margaret and Yado were in the officer's galley having a meal at sea when one of the pilothouse crew came rushing in and informed Chief Yado that the chadburn was broken. The crewman got Margaret's attention all right, but Yado never looked up from his meal and simply grunted an acknowledgement. After the crewman left, Margaret began to worry. She did not know what a chadburn was, but from the crewman's demeanor it was apparently important and it was broken! She began to think that the boat may be in danger of breaking in two and sinking and so she conveyed her fears to her newlywed husband. He simply told her that he would not get around to fixing the chadburn until he was darned good and ready and that would certainly not be before he finished

Margaret (Mahoney) O'Day and her son Gerald on the day of his high school graduation, June 24, 1942. Kevin O'Day Collection.

his dinner. A short tiff ensued and it was not until late in the argument that Margaret learned that a chadburn was simply a telegraph that signaled the engine room and its being broken would not cause the boat to sink–at least not out in mid-lake. Eventually, Yado did get around to fixing the chadburn, and he and Margaret did live happily ever after–although she never went sailing with him again.

Chief Simon O'Day, a.k.a. Yado, likely sailed on several boats in the Hutchinson fleet. Engineers of his era normally stuck to one company for their entire career and within that company they normally sailed on a limited number of the company's vessels. Unlike captains who tended to move from boat to boat, chiefs became wedded to their machinery and that is exactly the way the company wanted it. Often these engineers had their favorite boats and it is likely that Yado's favorite boat was not the *William A. Paine*, but rather it was

Chief Simon "Yado" O'Day and son Gerald just before Gerald was shipped off to World War II service. Kevin O'Day Collection.

the *J.J. Sullivan*. For many years and right up until his death on February 2, 1943 Yado kept a framed picture of the *Sullivan*. Even after his passing, whenever someone would see that picture and ask Margaret about it, the conversation would always lead to the retelling of the story of the *Richardson's* wreck. The story of Yado and the December shipwreck drama in which he was a player was told and retold and in that process the facts were changed, obscured and in large part omitted. Yet this was a very important event in the life and times of Chief Yado and it needed to be investigated and told in something close to its proper context. So it was that Kevin O'Day, a grandson that Yado never met, saw the picture and began to ponder the event and the shipwreck story in his

The photo of the J.J. Sullivan that hung on Yado's wall. *Kevin O'Day Collection.*

family lore. He contacted the author of this book and with a bit of Great Lakes detective work the story of Yado's shipwreck adventure was rediscovered. One mystery, however, still remains. That is the question of why his grandfather kept that picture of the *Sullivan*. Although the exact answer to that passed from this world with Yado himself, we can take a pretty good guess. Much like Margaret Mahoney, the *J.J. Sullivan* was probably favored by Chief O'Day because she was Irish.

The Frame's Floating Family Business

It was the eve of the Thanksgiving holiday of 1869 and three year old Jennie B. Houghton was just finishing her good night prayers. With tiny hands folded and eyes shut tightly the angelic little girl asked for a blessing upon her Mommy, Daddy, sister, Granny, Great Granny, and especially her Grandpa. Once the nightly prayers were concluded, Jennie crawled into the bed that she shared with her six year old sister Mary as their mom, Clarisia, proceeded to tuck the two children in for the night. For a long moment Jennie paused as if pondering a deep series of questions. Then, just as her mommy reached to turn off the oil lamp that illuminated the bedroom, the three year old spouted a before slumber question.

"When will Grandpa come home?"

"Soon," Clarisia responded.

"How soon?" Jenny persisted.

"As soon as his boat is finished working for the winter," her mother replied.

"Will that be in time for Thanksgiving tomorrow?" the little girl chirped hopefully.

"I don't think so," Clarisia replied. Then as she saw sadness enter into her child's eyes she added, "but you never know. There's always a chance he could surprise us."

"Do you think he will tomorrow?" Jennie gasped with sudden excitement.

"Probably not," Twisting the oil lamp's wick back and extinguishing the light Clarisia stopped the wave of excitement before it grew too large, "now go to sleep."

Outside of Jennie's bedroom window the late November wind moaned and brief hisses of snow pelted at the glass. The mind of a child shifts rapidly from one subject to another in the moments before sleep and Jennie's thoughts probably went from wanting her Grandpa to come home to the last time that he was at home. His strong hands lifting her onto his knee and his warm smile that was usually followed by a booming laugh were always a part of her memory of Grandpa being home. Whenever he would bring his boat, the scow-schooner *Volunteer*, into Ogdensburg harbor Jennie was allowed to play on deck. She was the apple of Captain Disbrow's eye and her presence on the boat was the seed that sprouted happiness. As the moments before sleep went on there were also the thoughts of the holiday to come. Although she did not recall much about the previous year's Thanksgiving, her grandma had been building up the excitement of this year's celebration to Jennie for several weeks. There would be a feast and all around the house an atmosphere of warm happiness. As Jennie drifted off to sleep, the thoughts of a happy Thanksgiving floated in her mind.

Captain Disbrow's boat was a born native of Lake Ontario and the St. Lawrence River. When she was constructed in Ogdensburg, New York in 1863 the *Volunteer* measured just 73 feet in length, 18 feet in beam and only 6 feet in depth. Although she seemed to be small by cargo vessel standards of her era, she had been built with a "scow bottom," that made her a practical cargo hauler. This flat bottom arrangement allowed her to be loaded with large amounts of cargo, yet still operate in shallow water. Additionally, her simple rigged twin masts allowed her to be manipulated by a crew of as little as two people. She went about her toil of hauling every sort of cargo that Captain Disbrow could arrange, to and from every port city on the Lake Ontario coast. She was not a spectacular beauty of the fresh water seas, but she was handy and inexpensive to operate. This season had required Jennie's Grandpa to keep his boat working late into November and capture a few additional loads to help pay for the long winter ahead when Lake Ontario's harbors would be encased in ice and the *Volunteer* would be tied to the dock. There was no chance that he would be home for Thanksgiving–no chance at all.

In the darkness of the autumn night Jennie suddenly awoke. There, standing at her bedside was her beloved Grandpa! Jennie was right, he had come home in time for the holiday. Excitedly she sat up in bed and stretched her arms out toward him.

"Grandpa!" she gasped in glee as she waited for him to sweep her up into his grasp.

But Grandpa Disbrow did not respond. He did not speak, he did not smile, he simply gazed down at Jennie with an unearthly sadness as the three year old flexed her fingers, enticing him to pick her up. Then the darkness of the room seemed to simply swallow him as he faded from her sight. Jennie was sure that her Grandpa was still in the room and she rolled over and began to shake her six year old sister Mary.

"Mary! Mary!" she urged in a whisper, "Wake up, Grandpa's here, light the lamp! Grandpa's here!"

With a grumble, Mary finally awoke and after some woozy listening she told her sister that there was no one in the room and to go back to sleep.

"You were dreaming," Mary groaned as she rolled over and pulled the blankets back up.

For a long time, Jennie stayed awake, waiting for Grandpa to return. Eventually she fell back into the blissful sleep that only a child can know. After all, when morning came, Grandpa would surely be there for the holiday feast and it would be an extra happy day. Maybe after dinner they would all go down to the dock and play upon the deck of the *Volunteer*. What Jennie could not know was that her Grandpa had indeed visited her, but in a strange and awful way that would haunt her for the rest of her life. The storm winds outside continued to moan as the three year old slumbered and many miles away the waves of Lake Ontario crashed and tumbled in a merciless rhythm.

Two dozen years after that Thanksgiving eve, the little scow-schooner *Volunteer* was still earning her living sailing the waters of the Great Lakes. Now under the ownership of Charles Henry Frame a 29 year old Canadian ex-patriot. Along with the rest of the Frame family, Charles had put down roots in the town of Sand Beach, Michigan in 1882 and now he was managing the operations of the *Volunteer*. The vessel was crewed by Charles' two brothers, 16 year old Herman, who was affectionately known as "Hermie" and 25 year old Burton. Working aboard the vessel as cook was Burton's wife, 18 year old Ida. Charles had placed the command of the vessel in the hands of his father, 57 year old John Frame. Together the Frame family operated the vessel as their family business, much the same as other families may operate a store or shop. The only difference was that the Frame family business floated and sailed from one port to another. Still the concept was the same, as Charles booked cargoes and kept the records straight, John ran the vessel and the other members of the family worked together to make the business profitable.

When Charles bought the *Volunteer*, he probably had little or no knowledge of the vessel's history. Scow-schooners such as the *Volunteer* were the pickup trucks of the waterways in the 1800s. The *Volunteer* was still as utilitarian as she had been in the days when Jennie's Grandpa had commanded the boat. To the Frame family the little boat seemed to have been built intending to do exactly the type of work that Charles had in mind. When he first came upon her as a prospective buyer he walked her decks, examined her rigging, checked her caulking and generally inspected her in the same manner that a small business owner today would inspect a new vehicle. He found her to be in worn, but in sturdy shape as well as being at the right price. With an exchange of cash the *Volunteer* was purchased and brought to Lake Huron. From then on she would serve as the Frame's floating family business. Charles had made a sensible deal on this tired old scow-schooner, however, he probably never bothered to check her for ghosts.

October of 1893 found the Frame's floating family business hard at work–hauling handy quantities of goods around the lakes. Back in Sand Beach, Charles had booked a trip that consisted of a modest cargo of $700 worth of freshly cut lumber that was to be loaded at Oscoda, Michigan and hauled to the metropolitan needs of Detroit. The cargo represented a tidy profit for the Frame family upon its delivery. This profit margin was supported by the fact that the additional cost of insurance on both the boat and its cargo was never taken. It was quite common for small operations such as this to gamble and run without insurance. However, it was a gamble that often proved to be disastrous.

When the *Volunteer* was loading at Oscoda, on the northwestern shore of Saginaw Bay, the weather had been deceptively calm. Captain Frame was sure that he could easily transport his load of lumber down to Detroit with little trouble. In fact his only concern may have been that there would not be enough wind to fill his sails as Lake Huron gave every indication of remaining flat calm. Fortunately, as the last of planks went aboard the little scow-schooner on Saturday afternoon October 14, 1893, enough breeze came up to huff the boat out of the slip and onto her course for Detroit. Ahead of the *Volunteer* lay 30 miles of open water before she could reach the nearest port of shelter which was Port Austin harbor. As the *Volunteer* wallowed into the expanse of Lake Huron and pressed on across the mouth of Saginaw Bay, the concern was more toward boredom than shipwreck. The winds were light and the scow-schooner was heavy, Captain Frame reasoned that it was going to be a long night and he was correct.

What Captain Frame could not know was that across the mitten state, over on Lake Michigan, a powerful gale had been ravaging the shipping lanes all day. Now those same storm winds were sweeping across the mainland of the lower peninsula and had their sights set on Lake Huron. Ahead of the approaching storm the climactic energies had built to the point where a dense fog had formed all around the *Volunteer* leaving Captain Frame to grope toward the course he thought to be correct. When the storm arrived on Saturday evening, its northeast winds caught the Frames and their floating family business in the worst possible position. The boat was just off the rocky reefs near Port Austin and Captain Frame may as well have hung out the "going out of business" sign right then and there. When he finally did get the Port Austin light in sight he found that he was well into the reefs. The only thing that had saved the little scow-schooner was her shallow draft. This characteristic now gave Captain Frame a fighting chance to get his boat back into deep water before she found an unfriendly boulder and had her bottom ripped out. Saving the *Volunteer* would, however, require tacking her into the wind that now blew as a full gale.

Through the night John, Burton and Hermie Frame fought to keep their vessel alive and watched as the lake systematically looted their cargo of lumber with each boarding wave. As the night grew late, the cargo was no longer their concern. Instead they thought only of remaining afloat until morning. As John held the boat's wheel, Burton and Hermie dashed between resetting the sails and working the boat's pumps. Below the *Volunteer's* decks the seams in her timbers gushed water and the vessel groaned as if about to go to pieces at any moment. Ice water sloshed in the tiny cabin as Ida Frame did her best to save their family possessions.

It became clear that the *Volunteer* could not be maneuvered against the wind and Captain Frame resigned himself to the fact that the only way to survive would be to drop the anchors and try to ride out the storm. Abandoning the wheel he went forward to help Burton and Hermie heave the giant hooks over the side. The men worked in a frantic effort to deploy the anchors before the winds could blow the boat onto the reefs of Michigan's thumb. In a drenched success, both hooks were dropped to the lake bottom and the *Volunteer* swung her head to the wind. For the moment they all thought that the vessel had a chance.

Through the remainder of the night, the Frame family spent their time bailing and working the boat's hand pumps. Often they prayed and just as often they wondered what was keeping the *Volunteer* afloat. From her condition, it was clear that she should have foundered and taken them all to their doom in hours ago, yet still she remained afloat. They all thought they would be happy to see the daylight, but contrary to their belief, the light of morning revealed just how bad their situation truly was. Through the night, the powerful winds and waves had caused the boat's anchors to drag and they were now being blown in toward the reefs near the shoreline. Now they began to debate launching the lifeboat and making a run for their lives through the deadly surf. No sooner had the Frame family debate over abandoning ship began than the *Volunteer* elected to make that decision for them. A groan rumbled from below decks followed by a thud and the boat suddenly twisted. Then a second shudder came from the bow and the boat began to drift. Her anchors had parted their chains and now the *Volunteer* was again in the clutches of Lake Huron.

Without further hesitation the Frame family mustered in the ship's yawl and abandoned the *Volunteer*. Rowing with all of their strength they headed toward the breakers. Surf such as this could easily capsize a small yawl boat such as theirs, yet they managed to stay upright and easily breeched the surf. The castaways managed to reach shore while taking little more than a good soaking along the way. As they dragged their tiny yawl onto the sandy beach between Hat Point and Oak Point, they watched the *Volunteer* crumble into a wreck on the reef just off shore. It was just after seven o'clock on Sunday morn-

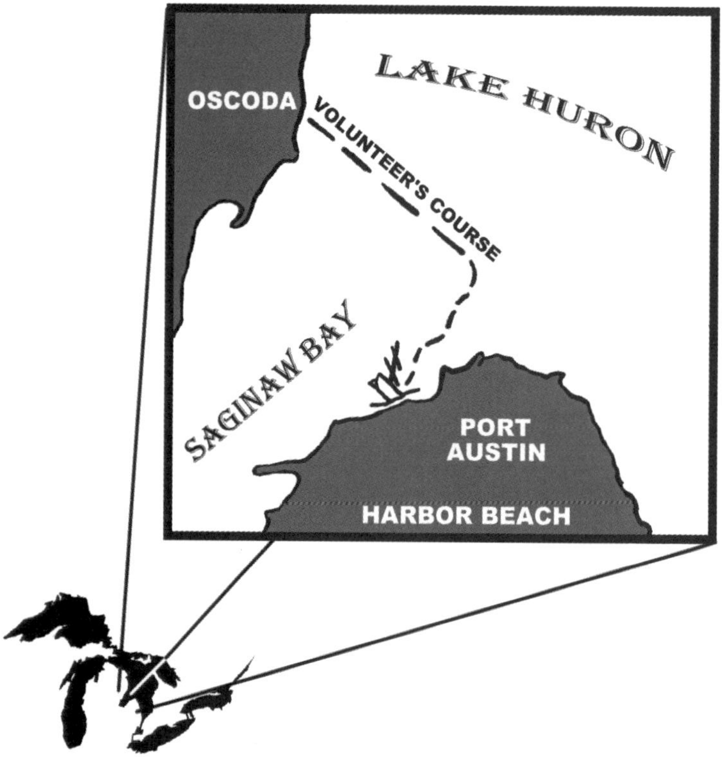

ing, October 15, 1893 and the entire Frame family felt as if some sort of miracle had just spared them from an icy death in Lake Huron. Of course, the walk along the lakeshore trail to Port Austin would be a long, cold 10 mile hike. No one knew to look back to see if a ghostly figure hovered near the wreck as the lake smashed the old scow-schooner to pieces.

The following morning Captain Frame went to the Port Austin life saving station and requested that the crew go with him to the wreck and see what could be saved. Launching their surfboat, the lifesavers pulled to the scene of the wreck with John, Burton and Hermie Frame as passengers. They found the *Volunteer* to now be nothing more than a shattered hulk with her lumber cargo scattered as far as the eye could see along the shore. All that could be salvaged from the boat itself was her rigging and sails. Then the lifesavers went out into the lake and dragged until they found her anchors which were also recovered. The estimated value of the boat and her cargo was $1,700. Overall the lifesavers recovered an estimated $400 worth of the *Volunteer* and her cargo. Local newspapers speculated that this disaster would be the end of the Frame's family maritime business, and they were right. Even worse, when the Huron Times gave an account of the wreck it described Herman Frame as the "...little son Hermie..." which must have really annoyed the 16 year old crewman. For the Frame family it seemed a disaster, yet any savvy vessel historian would look at it all and say that at least this time the *Volunteer* had spared her crew, unlike that Thanksgiving eve back in 1869. You see what little Jennie in the darkness at her bedside that night was not her Grandpa appearing to say "hello" instead he was there to say "goodbye."

As Jennie Houghton opened her eyes on Thanksgiving morning 1869, her first thoughts were to get out of bed and go find Grandpa. She remembered vividly the sight of him standing next to her bed during the night and now she was going to have the happiest of reunions with him. Surely he must be waiting for her to awaken and the sadness that he showed when standing at her bedside would melt away as soon as she hugged him.

In the kitchen, Jennie's mom, her grandma Mariah Disbrow and great grandma Clarissa Disbrow were already preparing the holiday feast. Jennie shuffled into the room and loudly asked, "Where's Grandpa?" Her mother tried to repeat the explanation of the previous evening saying that Grandpa was out sailing, but Jennie would hear none of it. She insisted that Grandpa was there. Then she caused every action in the kitchen to stop as she described his middle of the night appearance at her bedside in the matter-of-fact manner that only a child's innocence can manage. Grandma Disbrow was chilled with horror as the child went on and described the ghostly appearance and disappearance of her Grandpa. A feeling of dread settled down upon the household. In the hours that followed, none of the adults had much of an appetite for that Thanksgiving's feast. Their quiet Thanksgiving prayers were for the safe return of Captain Disbrow and they all felt that they would do their giving of thanks upon his return. Jennie did not understand why Grandpa was nowhere to be found in the household or why he had left and had not returned during that night. For the rest of the day she waited for him to come back. For the rest of her life she waited for him to come back.

That year's Thanksgiving holiday was one of two that did not fall on the fourth Thursday of the month of November, but instead was celebrated on November 18th. The following day the waterlogged wreck of the scow-schooner *Volunteer* was discovered washed up on the beach of Mexico Bay in the southeastern corner of Lake Ontario. In the days that followed items belonging to the vessel's crew began to wash up as well. Two carpet bags, a memo book with its contents smudged beyond being readable, an Enfield rifle and two silver rings–one inscribed "I.M.L." and the other inscribed "L.L." were all found in the area of the wreck. No bodies were ever found as Lake Ontario elected to keep Jennie's Grandpa and the rest of his crew forever. The *Volunteer*, however, was pulled from the beach by the tug *Crusader*. A crew then manned the boat's pumps and she was towed into Port Ontario. After extensive repairs the *Volunteer* went back into service. The news of the wreck did not get back to Jennie's family for another ten days.

Without doubt Mariah Disbrow wanted little to do with the vessel after the loss of her husband and thus the *Volunteer* began its pattern of being handed from one owner to another. Still the Great Lakes, especially Lake Ontario, seemed to go hard on the little scow-schooner. The 28th day of May, 1879 found the *Volunteer* becalmed about five miles off of the Big Sandy Life Saving Station on eastern Lake Ontario. Her crew had run out of food and the lifesavers had to shuttle out

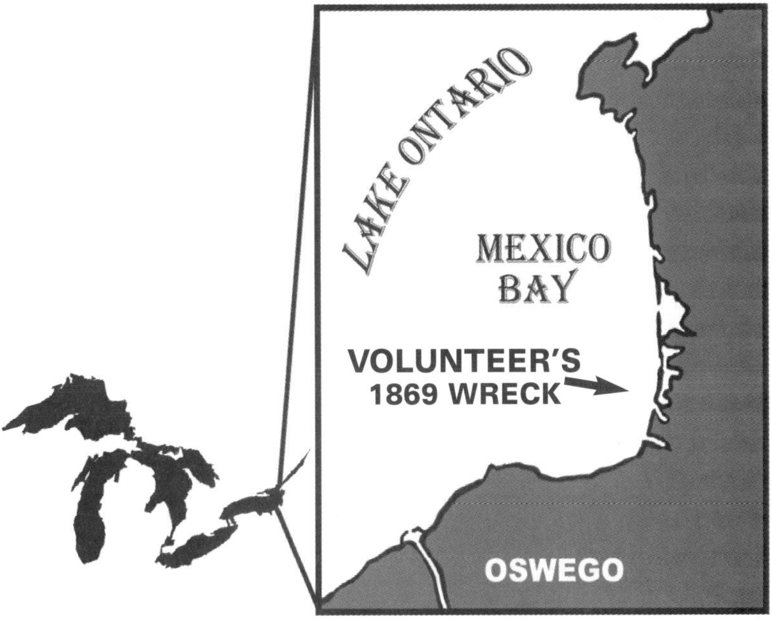

provisions to keep them from starving. The following day a breeze came up, but when the crew tried to take her into port she grounded and had to have her cargo lightened. Next, on August 15th of that same year, she stranded again at the mouth of Big Sandy, not far from where she had washed up after her wreck a decade earlier. No one was lost and the vessel was again towed in and repaired. Just a year later, on September 30, 1880 she again stranded in nearly the same location while trying to enter Port Ontario. This time her crew abandoned the boat and she stayed there for a full week before she could be salvaged. By the 1882 season, the *Volunteer* had passed from Lake Ontario owners to Cleveland owners and was engaged in hauling stone from Marblehead, Ohio. Lake Erie came along blowing a gale and sank the little scow-schooner at her Marblehead dock. That was her last brush with mishap until she wrecked on Michigan's thumb and finally ended the income from the Frame's floating family business.

No one knows exactly what happened to the crew of the *Volunteer* on that stormy Thanksgiving eve back in 1869. Either the boat was capsized and then later rolled back onto an upright keel, or was swamped and her people washed overboard or abandoned by her people who were then consumed by Lake Ontario while floundering in the lifeboat. The details of their end will forever be known to only those who were lost aboard her. Additionally, we do not know if the spirits of those who were lost aboard the *Volunteer* remained with the boat to watch over her for the next two dozen years. We do have the written account which says that before departing this world, Captain Disbrow summoned the power of his soul and traveled home to see his beloved granddaughter Jennie one last time to say goodbye.

True Tales Of Ghosts And Gales

As the sun set over Lake Huron on the evening of Wednesday, December 3, 1873, Captain Redmond Ryder looked toward the growing darkness with a watchful eye. The preceding day had been a taste of Indian summer as the lake remained calm and the air surrounding Captain Ryder's command, the downbound steamer *City Of Detroit*, had been still and almost hard to breath.

While most folks would be happy to see pleasant weather in the first days of December, the mariners of the Great Lakes know too well that this type of late season quiet means that big trouble is not far away. Leaving the pilothouse in charge of First Mate Daniel McIntyre, Captain Ryder also left orders that he was to be notified immediately if the wind came up one bit or if the seas turned into a dead swell. He then gave the mate a grim reminder that they were coming up on the mouth to Saginaw Bay, so the watch should especially beware of a wind out of the southwest. Mate McIntyre, like all of the *City Of Detroit's* crew knew full well why the captain held contempt for Saginaw Bay and winds from the southwest. It was a wound that ran so deep that no one aboard the *City Of Detroit* dared even to mention their understanding, they simply acknowledged the captain's directive and then allowed the matter to drop. That pain was so intense that the crew shared the captain's agony in spite of themselves. Everyone who served aboard the *City Of Detroit* knew of the unspoken tragedy that had been inflicted upon Captain Redmond Ryder courtesy of Saginaw Bay.

Captain Ryder was one of those "pioneer" steamboat masters who was among the few who had piloted a steamer upon Lake Superior before the Soo Locks had been constructed. In 1845, the steamer *Independence* had been dragged overland around the Saint Marys rapids and placed in service on Lake Superior. Initially, that famous steamer was captained by James Averill, but later the boat's command was taken by Redmond Ryder. This was an era on Lake Superior when the entire area was a northern wilderness where for most of the year the best means of transportation was by dog sled. There were few aids to navigation and the vast deposits of iron ore made a vessel's compass nearly useless. Steamboats of this period in time were in their early development and were prone to boiler explosions, fires and routine breakdowns. A steamer that was afflicted by such a problem would likely drift for days before being discovered or it may simply "go missing" never to be heard from again. Thus it took a special breed of mariner to be willing to command a steamer on the huge fresh water ocean known as Lake Superior, and Redmond Ryder was just such a steamboat man. In 1852, when the steamer *Baltimore* was portaged around the rapids and placed in Lake Superior's waters, Captain Ryder eventually found himself commanding her. Then in 1855 when the locks at Sault Saint Marie breached the rapids of the Saint Marys River and the shipping barons of the lower lakes saw their path to the riches of the great north opened, they went looking for steamboat captains who had Superior's ice water in their blood and Redmond Ryder was one of the primary captains selected. Commanding the propeller *General Taylor*, Captain Ryder made his first passage through the locks in 1856. By 1859, Captain Redmond Ryder was in command of the steamer *Mineral Rock* and making regular passages onto Lake Superior while the *General Taylor* was now under the command of his brother, Captain George Ryder. Indeed the Ryder family was one that had ice water in its blood. Over the years that followed, both of the Ryder brothers commanded a multitude of vessels and often when adventure was spawned on the upper lakes, one of them would almost certainly be found near to it.

Thus as Captain Redmond Ryder walked the deck of the *City Of Detroit* on that evening in 1873, each of his steps echoed with many years of experience sailing the Great Lakes. On his way aft to see what steward James Phelps was serving for dinner, Captain Ryder descended the stairs from the pilothouse and looked into the expanse of Lake Huron as it drifted past. The blue-gray water blended into the Indian summer haze. There was a quiet hiss as the *City Of Detroit's* bow splitting Lake Huron's surface. Beyond his thoughts of vessel business, payrolls, cargos and fuel stops there lurked the memories of his brother George. Painful images that lurked like shadows in his mind's eye. Images that haunted him every time he crossed this part of the lakes. Then there were those stories, always those blasted stories. They spread as rumors around the docks and taverns. Stories of a ghostly white steam ship with a red stack and a walking beam that ran athwart wise. In all of these stories, Redmond Ryder's brother was said to stand in command of the ghost ship as it plowed across Saginaw Bay seeking a safe port that was denied the vessel by an eternity. Such stories bothered Redmond Ryder because if they were nonsense then the mariners who spouted the yarns were drawing attention to themselves at the expense of his brother's fate. Worse yet, if the stories were true, that meant that his brother's soul was out there somewhere on Saginaw Bay, wandering in limbo.

Continuing on his way toward the *City Of Detroit's* galley, Captain Ryder turned his watchful eye aft toward the schooner-barge that his steamer was towing. Faithfully trailing behind the steamer came the *Guiding Star* with her rudder held so as to keep the schooner-barge out of the *City Of Detroit's* wake. Indeed, for late season sailing all looked to be in fine shape aboard both boats. Yet, as the door to the galley shut behind Captain Ryder, out there in the hazy distance across the surface of Saginaw Bay was the ghost that haunted him. It was the specter and the memory of a gleaming white steamboat with a red stack and a walking beam that operated in the wrong direction. The spirit of the fastest steamer on the lakes lurked out there. It was also the spirit of the proud brother of Redmond Ryder and the spirit of the steamer *Water Witch*. As the *City Of Detroit's* master tried to put the memory behind him in that Indian summer twilight in 1873, it had been exactly 10 years and 22 days since the *Water Witch* had passed from being a reality into being a ghost ship.

On the Great Lakes, a calendar turned to the date of November the 10th seems always to be a harbinger of disaster. Traditionally, that was a fact often ignored by the mariners as so it was that on that date in 1863 the steamer *Water Witch* departed Mackinaw City and headed down Lake Huron. The clock had just struck five o'clock in the evening when the shrill howl of the *Water Witch's* steam whistle echoed across the village and then was soaked up into the thick woods nearby. As the sound of the whistle bounced among the trees it was rapidly shredded by the powerful wind that ripped through the treetops baring them of any of the autumn leaves that had remained attached. Out on the water, the foul winds were churning the water into a rude gray chop that slapped at the stern of the steamer as she backed from the dock. Up in her pilothouse, the vessel's movements were being directed not by her captain, George H. Ryder, but by his first mate, George Beeman. Captain Ryder had taken ill and had relegated himself to his cabin. There is no record as to exactly what Captain Ryder's illness was, but we can assume that he must have been suffering greatly. It is very rare that the captains of vessels in this era relinquished command due to health, and thus the report that Captain Ryder had stepped down from his pilothouse is an indication that he was very ill indeed. Without doubt, all aboard knew that the sooner that the *Water Witch* got down to Sarnia and finished this trip, the better.

Beeman, along with the rest of the *Water Witch's* people had little concern caused by the weather and the lake that evening. The boat beneath their feet was just shy of two years old, and her builder, John L. Wolverton of Newport, Michigan had gone to great lengths to insure that she was innovative and beyond seaworthy. Her hull was staunchly planked and measured just short of 164 feet long. Across her deck was a measured beam of 25 feet four inches and she had a depth of nine feet four inches. In all her heavy oak hull timbers represented a formidable opponent to the winds and waves that the Great Lakes would throw at her. Located some 30 feet aft of her stem, the *Water Witch* had a special water-tight collision bulkhead. The heavy oak timbers of this bulkhead were inlaid with an India rubber lining and it was touted that even if the entire bow was destroyed in a collision, the boat could still remain afloat due to this bulkhead. Likewise, her capstan and windlass were geared to work together in another innovative detail. The real unique aspect of the *Water Witch*, however, was not in her forward accommodations, but in her engine workings.

A hint as to how different the propulsion of the *Water Witch* was could be seen from the outside. The huge walking-beam of her steam engine did not function by moving along the centerline of the vessel in a fore-and-aft direction as did every other steamboat on the Great Lakes, but rather the *Water Witch's* walking beam worked crossways to the boat or "athwartships" as the mariners described it. Down below, her steam engine was connected to the propeller shaft by way of a "cog-wheel." This allowed each stroke of the engine to be amplified on the propeller shaft and gave more turns of the propeller per stroke than other engines and thus higher speed.

It has been reported when she came out that the *Water Witch* could reach speeds as high as 18 mile per hour, yet most modern historians hold her in the 12 to 16 miles per hour range. The vessel's unique engine had been constructed at the Detroit Locomotive Works. Her boiler was probably the most ordinary piece of her hardware and had been constructed in Newport by the Messrs Brennan. Overall, however, the *Water Witch* was unlike anything on the lakes. The first reports of the vessel in service were published in late April of 1862, as an astonished maritime press discovered and then rapidly forgot her.

When the vessel assignments for the 1863 navigation season were announced, the Ryder brothers were each granted the honor of being in command of two of the newest boats on the lakes. Captain Redmond Ryder had given up his command of the steamer *Planet* and been given command of the brand new steamer *Meteor*. Captain George Ryder, who had been in charge of the steamer *Iron City* was given command of the one season-old steamer *Water Witch*. Thus one Ryder brother was to be the captain of the newest steamer on the lakes, while the other was to be in command of the fastest steamer on the lakes. We can only ponder the brotherly ribbing that went on prior to the beginning of the season as well as the greetings that were exchanged by megaphone between the two brothers each time that their vessels passed one another throughout the sailing season.

As darkness set in over the winds of Tuesday, November 10, 1863, the *Water Witch's* oil lamps seemed to be fighting a losing battle against the inky night. In the blackness she pitched and rolled but her new timbers hardly gave a squeak against the seas. Below in her engine room, Chief McCormick watched carefully over her eccentric engine. Her "cog" was a type of flywheel and the rest of the engine worked in a fairly normal manner. Still, the vessel had only been his to maintain for the past season, as she had just come into the employ of the E.B. Ward fleet at the opening of navigation. McCormick had expected her to be a handful, but soon learned that her odd ways were more of a help than a hindrance. Her cog wheel engine actually allowed for more efficient burning of fuel and thus McCormick's boys had to bring aboard the wood that she burned less often than they would have had to do on other steamers. Less fueling meant less work no matter how you looked at it. Other than the big flywheel, the engine had the same basic notches for insertion of the rod for shifting from forward to reverse and the same basic timing cams as other steam engines of the era. Tonight, the *Water Witch* was going up against Lake Huron and pounding her way to Port Huron as if the winds and waves were no match for her. In fact she would do that and make good speed of it too, or so thought McCormick.

By eight o'clock that evening, the *Water Witch* was just below Bois Blanc Island but had managed a speed of just seven miles per hour so far. At this point she was sighted by the propeller *Montgomery* and appeared to be making good weather of it. That apparently remained the case through the stormy night. By the time that the morning sky began to go from ink black to ink blue, the *Water Witch* was coming face to face with Saginaw Bay. The winds were now blowing a full gale from out of the southwest. It was the perfect direction to build big waves along the bay and then throw them at passing lakeboats often with deadly results. The *Water Witch* put her heavy oak bow into the seas and took each one as if to ask defiantly for the next.

Heading upbound was the bark *J.D. Norris*, with the same southwest gale at her heels and her sails filled with the storm. The *Norris* was making good time and good weather that morning and her crew were keeping a watchful eye on the horizon. The downbounders would be slow and she did not want to run anyone down. Off in the distance the *Norris'* crew spotted the distinct shape of the *Water Witch*. The steamer appeared to be dealing well with the storm and was about five miles away. Suddenly, in the wink of an eye and in a short few minutes when everyone aboard the *Norris* seemed to be somehow all looking away at the same time, the steamer with the red stack simply vanished. When everyone looked back in her direction the *Water Witch* was gone!

With a speed that only the crew of a sailing vessel can manage, the *Norris'* people scrambled up into her rigging to scan the distance for the missing steamer. Some thought that for a moment they saw her spar protruding above the waves, but other than that, there was nothing. The wind was blowing so hard that the *Norris* had no chance to alter her course and go in the direction of the missing steamer. In fact, the howling winds made it impossible to even hear much beyond the noise of the gale in the *Norris'* rigging. She sailed on up the lake with her crew left to wonder if what they had seen was a wrecked ship or a ghost ship. It turned out to be both.

In the days that followed, the *Water Witch* never reported to Sarnia. In fact, to this day she has never arrived in port. Eventually reports of wreckage being found floating in the lake began to come in. Five days after the steamer with the red stack had vanished in the mouth of Saginaw Bay, Captain Kenyon was bringing his command, the side wheel passenger steamer *Forest Queen*, around Michigan's thumb when a huge field of wreckage was encountered. Among the flotsam was a steward's desk with the drawers missing and all through the wreckage field were pieces of shattered cabins. While the *Forest Queen* was stopped in Port Austin, large pieces of the wreckage came ashore at that location. One piece was reported as having the initials "M.J.F." on it. This was probably the results of a little known, but recently rediscovered tendency of the Great Lakes crewmen of the wooden ship era. It seems that sailors of that generation were in the habit of carving their initials in the overhead timbers of the crew cabins. Thus, even though the *Water Witch* was less than two years old, apparently she had already been marked. There were also doors from a steamer that were coming ashore. These doors were painted on one side and wood grain on the other side. Every marine man that viewed the wreckage agreed that the carpentry which had been used to construct it was that which would be applied to the building of a steamer. All of the wreckage that was coming ashore was heavily splintered and shattered to the point that it was clear that some sort of explosion had caused them to be separated from their original structure. Most significant was the fact that the only vessel that was missing at that time, in that area was the *Water Witch*. At this same time, Captain Redmond Ryder was bringing the *Meteor* down from the upper lakes. On his way from Wellington Mines and hauling a load of 186 tons of copper ore that was consigned to be shipped to England, Captain Ryder had left his normal course and searched along the Canadian coast of Lake Huron in the hope that perhaps someone had escaped his brother's boat in a lifeboat. The lake was still running high and the wind was as bitter cold as Redmond Ryder's search. No trace of any survivor of the *Water Witch* would ever be found, in fact, no trace of anyone who had been aboard the vessel at the time of her loss would ever be found. The ice water of the Great Lakes had taken everyone, including Redmond Ryder's brother and it would never give them back.

Following the disappearance of the *Water Witch*, a rumor began to circulate along the docks and within the saloons of Saginaw, Bay City, Port Huron and eventually Detroit. The story was that while tossing a bucket of potato peelings overboard late one evening, a steward on a vessel sailing across Lake Huron was stunned to see another vessel passing much too closely to his own boat. But there had been no passing signal from his boat's whistle. The other vessel had no lights on and the steward thought that it was no wonder that the lookouts did not see her and hoot a passing signal. As he watched the large white steamer slide silently past he observed two distinct characteristics, she had a smoke stack painted red, and she had an odd looking walking beam …one that worked athwartships. The boat passed and then vanished right in front before his eyes.

This rumor would have no doubt soon fallen onto the ears of Captain Redmond Ryder and it is certain that every time he caught wind of it, the story involved some new mariner telling the same tale as if it had just happened. To Redmond Ryder the facts were far more clear than were the ghost ship stories. His brother's vessel had simply fallen victim to one of the most common mishaps in steamboating–a boiler explosion. The shattered wreckage, the sudden disappearance of the boat, all of the evidence pointed to this. In this era, boilers were often "backyard" productions. Their manufacturers were shops that sometimes built things other than boilers, but they could do a boiler if contracted. In other cases, the boilers were well built, but had simple structural or design flaws, and in many cases, inattention by the vessel's engineer allowed the water levels in the boiler to drop too low. The end result was always the same, an explosion, like a locomotive sized pipe-bomb. Normally, these boiler explosions nearly leveled the vessel and often killed everyone aboard instantly. Perhaps that was the one fact that helped Redmond Ryder to rise above the grief of the loss of his brother. He knew that in a boiler explosion there would be no suffering as in the cold fate of drowning. Yet if indeed his brother's lost spirit were to be still sailing out there on Lake Huron, he would indeed be suffering. Perhaps if Redmond could see the ghost ship itself, he could help to guide his brother to the safe port that was his just reward.

It is likely that on that Indian summer evening in December 1873 as Redmond Ryder made his way toward dinner, the thought of his lost brother and what Lake Huron had done on that black morning ten years ago, crossed his mind. It was a ghost that seemed to haunt him and everyone around him. Tonight, however, the *City Of Detroit's* master had a bigger concern that was also pressing upon him. Being a Great Lakes mariner of long experience, he knew well that balmy weather this time of the year meant that bad things were going to start happening and that change in weather would likely come without warning. Anytime that the normal crisp late season temperatures are replaced by spring-like conditions it is a precursor of the lakes about to let loose a gale of considerable power.

Back behind the *City Of Detroit*, Captain Morris Barrett was in command of the grain laden schooner-barge *Guiding Star*. He too saw the weather as a lurking monster. The *Guiding Star* had taken her cargo of 24,000 bushels of grain at Milwaukee, and now Captain Barrett was crossing his fingers in the hope that the *City Of Detroit* could haul them both into the protected waters of Sarnia before the weather cut loose. He figured that they should be off of the Ft. Gratiot light and safe by about half past three o'clock the next afternoon ...he was wrong.

The squall line that preceded the mass of arctic air sweeping down from the northwestern plains was filled with powerful thunderstorms complete with lightening, tornados, hail and hurricane force winds. Moving at more than 40 miles per hour, the storm front came from the southwest. In the city of Saginaw, Michigan, inland and some 70 miles south of the *Guiding Star* and *City Of Detroit's* location, the squall hit at about two o'clock in the morning. It started with a driving rain that was ice cold followed in rapid succession by lightening, hail and then the powerful wind. The temperature began to fall at the rate of one degree per minute and fell from near 70 degrees to 18 degrees. Many folks had left their windows open to enjoy the late season's fresh air and as the wind came up it took advantage of these openings. Blasting through homes, slamming doors, shattering some windows and simply blasting others out of their frames the wind hit like an explosion. Brick chimneys were toppled and trees up-rooted as the storm roared through the city. On the corner of Cass and William streets a development called "The Brick Block" owned by Thomas R. Mosher and consisting of a number of nearly finished brick buildings was simply blown over like so many dominos. On the Saginaw River the scene was complete chaos. Most vessels had been laid up for the winter and although their lines were secure, there was no ice in the river to hold their hulls. When the winds came up, the idled vessels were scattered like chips on a pond. The barge *General Sherman* was blown against the Genesee Street bridge, impacting hard. It had been followed by a floating pile-driver which not only hit the bridge, but had also been tipped over and sunk. On the west foot of the bridge the house of the boat club was picked up by the wind and thrown into the river. The bridge tender's cab was torn from the bridge and tossed onto the piles below. Fortunately, the bridge tender had been retired for the season and was not on duty at the time. The tug *Eya* was blown over and began to fill with water. Luckily, her master was living aboard and enlisted aid from folks on the docks to help him try to pump her out. At the train depot three imported French plate glass windows were blasted in by the wind. All over the city anything that the wind could take advantage of, it destroyed.

Swooping up from the southwest the storm made its way up the mitten of Michigan and toward Lake Huron. On the way it struck Bay City and the massive fleet of wooden lakeboats that were hibernating there for the winter. The barge *C.N. Ryan* was broken from her moorings and sent along the waterfront unmanned and out of control only to slam into the Sherman Coal dock. The propellers *Bradbury* and *Saginaw* were also broken from their docks and then slammed into the D&B railroad bridge. In the same confusion the tug *Buffalo* was ripped lose and sent toward the F&PM railroad bridge, but drifted aground before reaching the structure. Not so lucky was the tug *McDonald*, which was drifting along behind the *Buffalo*. With her crew off for the winter lay-up, the *McDonald* was now torn from her dock and under the control of the storm. Without a moments regret the winds took the tug and shoved her right under the heavy iron railroad bridge. When the tug met the bridge, there was the sound of shattering cabins and bending steel as the vessel's deck houses were ripped off and her smokestack was bent over. Of course the winds decided to take that moment to let go and leave the poor *McDonald* wedged under the bridge. Ashore at the Bay City opera house the wind blew in the plate glass window. Once it had gotten access to the opera house, the wind then proceeded to blow inside, lift off a section of the roof directly over the stage and toss the roofing across the street. The gale then danced upon the stage and howled its song of stormy opera to seats filled with swirling zephyrs of breeze that whistled "bravo."

Damage similar to that seen in Saginaw and Bay City was caused all around the lower lakes from Chicago to Toronto as the massive system of arctic air swept away the warm air of Indian summer. Now the winds that could plunder whole cities set their sights on two small lakeboats out on open Lake Huron. For the *Guiding Star* and *City Of Detroit* there would be no escape. It is doubtful that the lookouts on either vessel saw the squall line approaching. The thick and humid conditions that made up the air mass ahead of the cold front would have obscured visibility to the point where even the lightening of the thunderstorms would have been imbedded and hidden in the darkness. There may have been the distant rumbles of thunder, but little more than that would have provided any warning. The two vessels were hauling along on a glass smooth lake in spring-like conditions as Captain Barrett snoozed lightly in his bunk aboard the *Guiding Star*. Just past 3:30 in the morning he was awakened by the hiss of driving rain on his window. Making his way to the companionway, he saw William Dean at the wheel, drenched and squinting into the rain. Captain Barrett took the wheel himself and ordered his crew of three to batten down and get ready for heavy weather. Just how heavy it was about to become was far beyond Captain Barrett's imagination.

Moments behind the rain came the blasts of wind unlike anything that Captain Barrett had witnessed in his entire career on the lakes. In fact, the *Guiding Star* and *City Of Detroit* could not have been in a worse position to be ravaged by the storm. They were directly in the mouth of Saginaw Bay and the storm had fifty miles of open water to turn into massive waves to throw at the two wooden lakeboats. In the space of just a few hours the waves were towering nearly 30 feet high and the *Guiding Star* and *City Of Detroit* were fighting just to stay afloat. In short order, the *City Of Detroit* had abandoned her course to Sarnia and was simply being headed into the wind with the *Guiding Star* trailing behind her like the tail of a kite.

Dawn arrived like a bill collector seeking a final payment from the Ryder family. By the time that the sky began to show the gray daylight the storm clouds were moving overhead with a deadly swiftness and the *City Of Detroit* was fighting for her life as well as for the life of Captain Barrett's *Guiding Star*. Laboring heavily, the steamer suddenly cut the schooner-barge lose. As the barge began to drift leeward of the steamer and Captain Barrett's three crewmen scrambled to rig her musty storm sail, he took notice that the *City Of Detroit* was also adrift. It was then that a shocking realization came over Captain Barrett. The hefty form of the *City Of Detroit* presented a lot more area to the wind than did the *Guiding Star*, and now the wind was shoving the big steamer directly toward the little schooner-barge. At just 324 tons, the *Guiding Star* was exactly half the mass of the *City Of Detroit*, and the big steamer could easily run her down. All that the four men aboard the schooner-barge could do was to hold on and watch as the storm blew the *City Of Detroit* in their direction. Passing nearly within shouting distance of the *Guiding Star* the *City Of Detroit* narrowly missed colliding with her barge. As the steamer passed, the crew of the *Guiding Star* clearly saw their counterparts assembling on deck. The entire crew of the *City Of Detroit* appeared to be gathered at the vessel's stern. A few of the steamer's people appeared to be preparing to launch the lifeboat, but most appeared to be simply standing there gazing off into the distance. As if they saw salvation on its way toward them. It was a sight that drove a simultaneous shiver up the spines of the crew of the *Guiding Star*. It was as if those inanimate crew members of the *City Of Detroit* were already dead.

Shortly after the helpless steamer passed the *Guiding Star*, the schooner-barge's crew witnessed the *City Of Detroit's* lifeboat lowered into the towering waves. Although the *Guiding Star* herself was being tossed in seas that towered nearly as high as her gaff, the crew were able to see at least three of the *City Of Detroit's* people get away in the lone lifeboat. A heartbeat later the *City Of Detroit* lurched astern and went to the bottom of the lake like a sack of coal. The place where she went down is almost the exact same location where Captain Redmond Ryder's brother George had been lost with his vessel, the *Water Witch* ten years and 23 days earlier. The *Guiding Star* shook in a frightening manner as a sickening rumble thundered from the lake. So close had the sinking *City Of Detroit* been to the schooner-barge that her suction actually reached out and trembled the *Guiding Star*. In the distance, for only a few minutes, the lifeboat and its helpless castaways could be seen. They apparently had only one oar, and one crewman was attempting to pull with it while the other two slapped themselves in an effort to stay warm. Before the witnesses on the *Guiding Star* were forced to watch too much of the lifeboat crews, suffering winds had carried

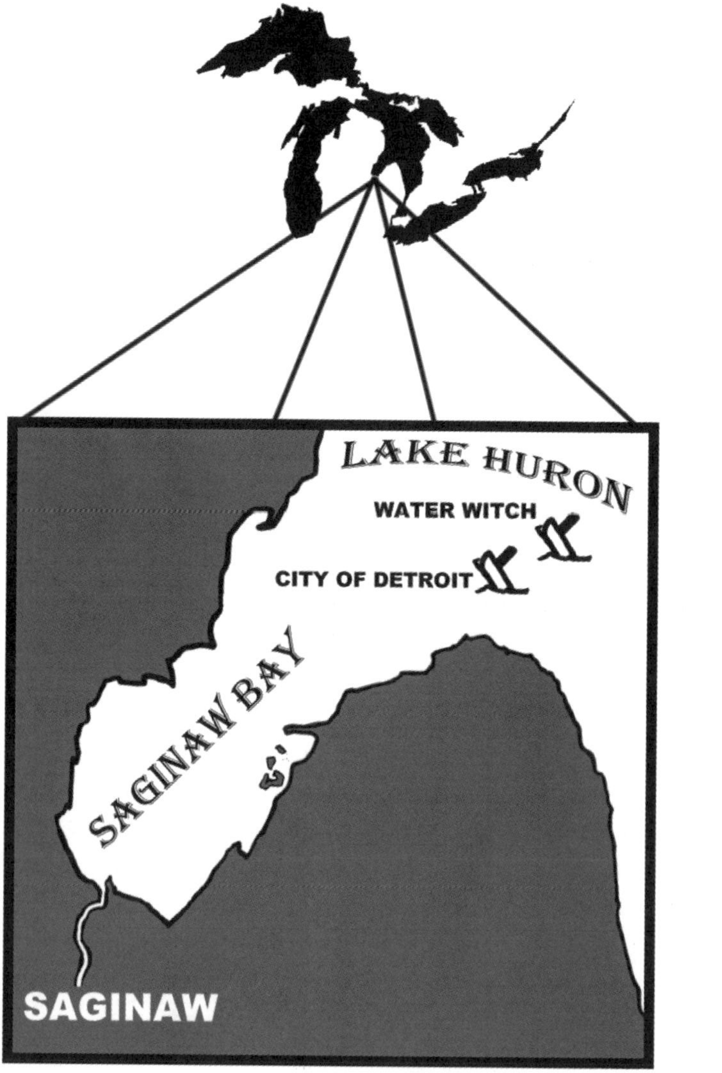

them away to meet their fate in another of Lake Huron's unmarked graves. The *Guiding Star* was then alone in the gale.

Captain Barrett now turned his attention toward saving his own vessel. The task of setting the storm sail was impossible. Temperatures were now well below freezing and rapidly dropping toward the teens, so every drop of water that splashed or sprayed upon the *Guiding Star* was instantly freezing. Worse yet it had been raining and the canvas had been soaked. Thus the rigging needed to raise her sail was frozen solid as was the sail itself. The crew had their hands benumbed by the cold and were unable to work her lines. Finding six inches of water in the boat's hold sloshing around with her grain cargo, the *Guiding Star's* crew now took to her pumps. These wooden hand pumps were located on the exposed deck and so crewmen William Dean, George Dawes and one who is identified simply as "Poland" took turns working the pump.

For endless hours the storm blew the *Guiding Star* helplessly toward the Canadian coast as the waves washed over both her and her crew. The cabins were filled with water and although the hold still had about a half a foot of Lake Huron in it, the lake was not apparently gaining on the boat. Incredibly, it was reported that the *Guiding Star* drifted, wallowing in the waves from Thursday morning until Saturday morning. By that time the schooner-barge came within sight of land, and Captain Barrett elected to take to the vessel's yawl and make for shore. Both he and his crew were suffering badly from frozen feet and hands and this late in the season, the next friendly boat may not pass until spring. With that thought in mind the desperate crew of the *Guiding Star* took to the lifeboat and abandoned their vessel about nine miles off of the Canadian shore. By Saturday afternoon, they were in Port Elgin, Ontario and rapidly recovering from Lake Huron's frosty touch of death.

On Sunday morning, a tug was dispatched and the waterlogged *Guiding Star* was recovered. She would continue to serve on the lakes until the white hurricane of November 5, 1883 when she would be wrecked a dozen miles north of Milwaukee on Lake Michigan. Captain Barrett and the rest of his crew also survived and went on to further adventures on the Great Lakes. Each of them, however, carried with them the memory of those faces of the lost mariners aboard the floundering *City Of Detroit* as it was carried past them in the storm of December 4, 1873. Oddly, after the loss of Redmond Ryder and his boat, the reported sightings of his brother's ghost ship seemed to suddenly stop. Still for the *Guiding Star's* survivors there was something about the look in the eyes of those doomed crewmen that continued to haunt them. Perhaps the *City Of Detroit's* crewmen saw their own end coming. Or perhaps they were in shock that the lake had overcome their grand vessel. Or perhaps they too had caught a glimpse of that white steamer with a red smoke stack and a walking beam that works athwartships. A steamer that sails forever on Saginaw Bay between reality and eternity. Maybe instead of Captain Redmond Ryder guiding his long lost brother George, the *Water Witch* and it's crew to their just reward, perhaps George had brought the *Water Witch* to guide the *City Of Detroit* and her people to their eternity.

About The Author

W. Wes Oleszewski
Great Lakes Maritime Author and Research Historian. Photo by Roger Nelson

Author W. Wes Oleszewski was born and raised in mid-Michigan and spent most of his life with an eye turned toward the Great Lakes. In the past 11 years he has authored 10 books on the subject of Great Lakes maritime history and lighthouses.

Noted for his meticulous research, Oleszewski has a knack for weeding out the greatest of details from the most obscure events and then weaving those facts into the historical narratives which are his stories. His tales of actual events are real enough to thrill any reader while every story is technically correct and highly educational. Oleszewski feels that the only way to teach history in this age of computer and video games is through "narrative." Along the researcher's path this author has also become acquainted, sometimes first-hand, with the multitude of ghosts and ghost stories that haunt the history of the lakes. The final product of his efforts are captivating books that can be comfortably read and enjoyed by everyone from the eldest grandmother to the grade school kid and future historian.

His most recent projects include the definitive study of the forgotten shipwrecks located in the Saginaw River and a production of CDs for computer viewing that detail the study. Additionally, Wes is working with representatives of the University of Michigan in a documentation and study of the shallow water shipwrecks of the Great Lakes, the results of which will be placed into computer accessible form on CD as well as on the Internet where the public at large can view the study in progress. Also he has been aboard the luxury cruise ship *C. Columbus* in the autumn of 2000 to act as a guide to the Great Lakes and give lectures.

Born on the east side of Saginaw, Michigan in 1957, Wes Oleszewski attended public school in that city through grade nine, when his family moved to the town of Freeland, Michigan. In 1976 he graduated from Freeland High School and a year later entered the Embry-Riddle Aeronautical University in Daytona, Florida. Working his way through college by way of his own earned income alone, Oleszewski graduated in 1988 with a commercial pilot's certificate, "multi-engine and instrument airplane" ratings as well as a B.S. Degree in Aeronautical Science. Along with his writing, he has pursued a career as a professional pilot. He holds an A.T.P. certificate and to date has logged more than 5,000 hours of flight time most of which is in airline category and jet aircraft. In 2000, Wes "retired" from flying and "went pro" as an author and lecturer. Samples of his work can be found on his web site at www.lighthouses-lakeboats.com.

Glossary

Abeam: Directly beside a vessel
Aft: Toward the rear of a vessel
Back: A ship's spine or keel
Barge: A vessel that has no power of its own and must be towed
Beam: The width of a vessel
Beam ends: The sides of a vessel
Boat: On the Great Lakes, a ship is called a boat
Bulkhead: A wall-like partition that divides a boat's hull
Bunker: A compartment where a boat's fuel is stored
Capstan: Device used for pulling lines or chains
Firehold: The part of the engine room where the boiler fires are fed
Fo'c'sle: The raised part of a boat's bow containing crew quarters
Founder: To sink in a disastrous way
Funnel: A steamer's smokestack
Hawser: A tow line, steel or rope
Heel: To lean to one side
Keel: A supporting beam that runs the length of a boat's bottom
List: A tilt to one side
Lighter: To raise a sunken boat by removing its cargo
Port side: Left side
Saltie: An ocean going vessel that visits the lakes
Schooner-barge: A sailing vessel that is usually towed
Screw: Propeller
Spardeck: The maindeck through which cargo is loaded
Texas deck: The deck atop which the pilothouse is mounted
Yawl: A small rowboat or lifeboat

Bibliography

A Voice In The Fog
Ref:
Milwaukee Sentinel, 9/10, 15, 16, 17, 18, 19, 20, 21/1873
Saginaw Daily Courier, 9/16, 17, 18/1873, 11/6/1873
Milwaukee City Directory, 1873-1874
Detroit Free Press, 9/21/1864
"Freshwater Whales" Wright
Letter correspondence with Suzette Lopez, Milwaukee Public Library, 9/11/2002
Boatnerd.com, News section, 8/8/2000
Telephone interviews with U.S. Coast Guard personnel conducted autumn of 2000, names, dates and stations withheld upon request, no written record maintained upon request.

Midnight *and* Mears
Ref:
Saginaw Courier Herald, 4/22/1887, 12/3,4,7/1889
Saginaw Evening News, 12/5, 7/1889
Bay City Tribune, 12/1, 3, 4/1889
Bay City Daily Tribune, 11/8, 10, 12, 14/1888
United States Life Saving Service Annual Report, 1890
"Wreck Ashore" Stonehouse
"The U.S. Life Saving Service, Heroes, Rescues and Architecture of the Early Coast Guard" Shanks & York
"The U.S. Life Saving Service-1880" Merryman

List of Merchant Vessels of the United States, 1889
Classification of Lake Vessels, 1871
E-mail correspondence with Dr. John O'Shea, 5/22/2002

The Haunting Of Hugh McKenna
Ref.:
Port Huron Times, 11/10, 12, 13, 14, 15, 16, 19, 20, 21, 23/1901
Merchant Vessels of the United States, 1915
"Our Inland Seas Their Shipping and Commerce," Mills
"Freshwater Whales," Wright
Great Lakes Vessels Index, Historical Collections of the Great Lakes, Bowling Green State University

Let Her Perish
Ref:
Oswego Palladium, 11/29/1878
Annual Report of the United States Life Saving Service, 1879
"Wreck Ashore" Stonehouse
"The U.S. Life Saving Service, Heroes, Rescues and Architecture of the Early Coast Guard" Shanks & York
"The U.S. Life Saving Service-1880" Merryman
"The Bay of Dead Ships" Reich
"Images of America, Around Oswego" Prior & Siembor
Dave Swayze database
E-mail correspondence with research historian Richard Palmer, 12/14/1997

Bones In The Backwaters
Ref.:
Saginaw Daily Courier, 7/15, 26, 27, 29, 31/1873, 8/10, 15/1873, 10/22, 23, 31/1873, 11/2/1873
Bay City Tribune, 12/21/1910
Port Huron Times, 11/3/1872
Bay City Times, 1/31/1982

Polk's Bay City Directory, 1868/1869 (Miscellaneous section), 1873-1874, 1874-1875, 1896,
"History of Bay County," 1883
"Bay County Past and Present," Butterfield
"Handbook for Shipwrights," Davis
Dave Swayze shipwreck data base
E-mail correspondence with Dave Swayze, 1/17/2001
E-mail correspondence with Dr. John O'Shea, 11/15/2000
E-mail correspondence with Patrick Labadie, 1/30,31/2001
Letter correspondence with the Bay City Branch Library, 2/14/2001

Escape From Murray's Nightmare

Ref.:
Port Huron Weekly Times, 5/11/1871
Dave Swayze Database
E-mail correspondence with Research Historian Dave Swayze, 2/22/2002
Michigan Family History Network web site
"Lake Superior Shipwrecks" Wolff
"Lake Superior's Shipwreck Coast" Stonehouse
Kingston Daily News, 10/14/64
J.W. Hall 1871 Wreck List
"Steaming Through Fire and Ice" Donahue
Author's visit to Whitefish Point, 8/2001

Almost Ghosts

Ref.:
Author's visit to Superior, WI, 8/22/01
"The Huron Heritage" Stark
"A Pictorial History of the Great Lakes" Hatcher & Walter
"Know Your Ships 2002" LeLievre
"Queen of the Lakes" Thompson
"The New Namesakes of the Great Lakes" Greenwood
Ship Masters Association Directory, 1948

Calls To Duty
Ref:
Huron Times, 6/1/1889
Annual Report of the United States Life Saving Service, 1888, 1889, 1890
"Wreck Ashore" Stonehouse
"The U.S. Life Saving Service, Heroes, Rescues and Architecture of the Early Coast Guard" Shanks & York
"The U.S. Life Saving Service-1880" Merryman
Dave Swayze shipwreck database
Detroit Post and Tribune, 8/11/1882

Yado
Ref.:
Buffalo Courier Express, 12/9/1909
Buffalo Commercial, 12/9, 10, 11, 13, 14/1909
Lorain Times Herald, 12/10, 11, 12/1909
Letter correspondence from Kevin O'Day 3/8/1997, 4/19/1998, 9/22/2002
Correspondence with the Buffalo and Erie County Public Library 5/27/1998
Great Lakes Vessels Index, Bowling Green State University
"Lighthouse Adventures," Oleszewski
"Ghost Ships of the Great Lakes," Boyer
"100 Best Great Lakes Shipwrecks," Kohl
Dave Swayze Database

The Frame's Floating Family Business
Ref.:
Huron Times, 10/20, 27/1893
Oswego Daily Advertiser, 11/28/1869
Toledo Blade, 11/20/1869
Dave Swayze Database
USLSS Annual Report, 1879,1880,1881,1883,1894
"Rock Falls Cemetery Sand Beach Township Huron County

Michigan" LaBelle
"Portrait of a Village: Port Hope Huron County, Michigan" Smith and Hunter
Michigan Family History Network web site
Federal Census of St. Lawrence County, 1870
"History of the Great Lakes" Mansfield
"Wreck Ashore" Stonehouse
"Directory of the Marine Interests of the Great Lakes" Polk, 1884
"Classification of Lake Vessels and Barges" Adopted by a Board of Marine Inspectors, April 1, 1871, Warren, Johnson & Co. 1871
Association of Canadian Lake Underwriters, Lake Vessel Register, Toronto: W. C. Chewett & Co., 1866. Canadian ship classification list.
"List of Merchant Vessels of the United States" 1884
Excerpt from the unpublished work "Pioneer Families of Eastern Huron County" by Dale L. Burley. Information on John Frame transcribed and sent by e-mail from Diana Hebner of the Huron Genealogical Society, 7/20/2002
Author's visit to the wreck site, 7/19/2002

True Tales Of Ghosts And Gales

Ref:
Detroit Free Press, 4/27, 30/1862 11/16, 17, 18, 19/63, 4/14, 19/1864, 11/20/1874
Cleveland Morning Leader, 11/19/1863
Saginaw Daily Courier ,7/15/1873, 12/5, 6, 7, 11/1873
Bay City Morning Chronicle, 12/5, 6, 7, 9, 10, 11/1873
Cleveland Plain Dealer, 12/5, 8/1873
Port Huron Daily Times 12/4, 8, 9, 11/1873
Kingston Daily News, 12/4/1863
"Lake Superior Shipwrecks" Wolff
"Graveyard of the Lakes" Thompson
"The Honorable Peter White" Williams

E-mail correspondence with Dave Swayze, 2/25/1998, 3/8/1998, 1/11/1999, 8/12/1999, 10/6/00
E-mail correspondence with Brendon Baillod, 4/23/1998
E-mail correspondence with Andy Donato, 1/12/200
E-mail correspondence with C. Patrick Labadie, 3/5/1998
Letter correspondence with the Great Lakes Historical Society, fact sheet on the wreck of the *Water Witch*
The Scanner, Vol. XIII, April 1981

Other Wes Oleszewski titles by Avery Color Studios, Inc.

- *Stormy Disasters,*
  Great Lakes Shipwrecks
- *Ice Water Museum*
  Forgotten Great Lakes Shipwrecks
- *Ghost Ships, Gales & Forgotten Tales*
  True Adventures On The Great Lakes
- *Mysteries and Histories,*
  Shipwrecks of the Great Lakes
- *Great Lakes Lighthouses,*
  American & Canadian
- *Lighthouse Adventures*
  Heroes, Haunts & Havoc
  On The Great Lakes
- *Keepers Of Valor, Lakes of Vengeance,*
  Lakeboats, Lifesavers & Lighthouses